AFTER
PURITY

AFTER PURITY

RACE, SEX, AND RELIGION
IN WHITE CHRISTIAN AMERICA

SARA MOSLENER

BEACON PRESS
BOSTON, MA

BEACON PRESS
24 Farnsworth Street
Boston, Massachusetts
www.beacon.org

Beacon Press books
are published under the auspices of
the Unitarian Universalist Association of Congregations.

28 27 26 25   8 7 6 5 4 3 2 1

This book is printed on acid-free paper that meets the uncoated paper
ANSI/NISO specifications for permanence as revised in 1992.

Text design and composition by Kim Arney

Portions of chapter 7 have been previously published in
"White Women's Bodies and the Dilemma of Purity Culture," *The Revealer*,
February 7, 2023, https://therevealer.org/white-womens-bodies-and
-the-dilemma-of-purity-culture-recovery/.

*Library of Congress Cataloging-in-Publication
Data is available for this title.*
ISBN: 978-0-8070-1499-8; e-book: 978-0-8070-1498-1;
audiobook: 978-0-8070-1835-4

The authorized representative in the EU for product safety and compliance
is Easy Access System Europe 16879218, Mustamäe tee 50,
10621 Tallinn, Estonia: http://beacon.org/eu-contact.

To Fay Botham
1968–2021
Scholar of religion and race, friend,
and menace to Christianity.

I miss you.

CONTENTS

FOREWORD

Many of the girls I grew up with in my White, Midwestern, evangelical Christian church dreamed of one day becoming a pastor's wife.

Not a pastor.

Women weren't *allowed* to be *pastors*. Hell, women weren't even allowed to be head *usher* at *my* church! That would require telling the other volunteer ushers what week they were scheduled, and no woman was going to tell a man what to do if *my* church had anything to say about it.

Having internalized these limitations, the girls I grew up with learned to dream less about *being someone* than about being *adjacent* to someone. The number 2 to his number 1. Soft, silent, sweet, and *so close to the top*.

But not me.

I wanted to be a missionary.

Because I knew that out there on the missions field, the gender-based rules that structured my life simply didn't apply. Working with Black and Brown folks overseas, women like me could lead. We could teach. Sometimes, we could even preach!

Though I didn't recognize it until years later, the logic was obvious to anyone willing to look: within my religious community, my supposed White, Western European *su*periority superseded my presumed gender-based *in*feriority.

As anecdotes such as this illustrate, nationalism, colonialism, and White supremacy are woven into the fabric of White, American evangelical Christian cultural theology, including its purity-branded teachings on gender and sexuality. And, yet, in the words of the author of the crucial book you hold in your hands, Dr. Sara Moslener, "our current historiography of sexual purity is framed within debates over gender and sexuality alone." *After Purity* expands this overly simplistic version of the story—delving deeply into the intersection of White supremacy and evangelical Christian purity culture.

Over twenty years ago, before the term "purity culture" even existed, Moslener and I were both researching the topic—she on the West Coast, and I on the East Coast—though we didn't meet until ten years later. Impressed by her first book, *Virgin Nation*, and eager to meet another purity culture scholar during a time in which few existed, I cold-called Moslener in 2017.

I immediately regretted not having done so sooner.

In the years that followed, Moslener became one of my most trusted colleagues. We bounced ideas off each other, planned projects together, and confided in one another when the work was hard—and it is often hard.

I went on to publish my book *Pure: Inside the Evangelical Movement That Shamed a Generation of Young Women and How I Broke Free*. I also launched a nonprofit that connected individuals raised in purity culture to one another and supported them in sharing their stories, and I developed a coaching practice serving purity culture survivors, among other things.

Moslener, meanwhile, coedited an anthology of essays on purity culture, cofounded the Post-Purity Healing and Recovery database with Liv Schultz, codeveloped Writing Religious Wrongs with Cait West and Dawn Burns, cochaired the Religion and Sexuality Unit of the American Academy of Religion, participated in the Luce Foundation's Religion and Sexual Abuse Project, and much more.

You may notice a theme in the list: that recurrent "co-." Moslener is a *collaborator*.

So, when she told me that she was going to write a book about race, sex, and religion—having taught about racism and discrimination in religion at Central Michigan University for over a decade and having hosted the *Pure White* podcast on the same topic—I knew she'd bring her signature collaborative spirit to the work. True to form, Moslener worked with womanist and Black feminist thought leaders like Dr. Monique Moultrie and Dr. Kaisha Esty, refining her thinking toward the development of a critical contribution to the field of purity culture studies.

Sexualization and its counterpart *de*sexualization are well-worn tools of racism. In American culture, women of color are generally sexualized, and violence against them is too often justified based on malicious sexual stereotypes. Many men of color are also sexualized, such as Black men who are framed as dangerous and needing to be controlled in order to protect White women. At the same time, other men of color, such as Asian men, have been historically *de*-sexualized to emphasize White male superiority.

Enter into this vicious mix the so-called Pure White Woman.

Moslener takes us back to the nineteenth century, when the Victorian gender roles that so deeply inform today's purity culture were introduced. It is then, she writes, that the historical Christian denouncement of women as little more than seductresses is complicated by the introduction of a new category: the "pure," wealthy, White, religious woman with no interest in sex or other such frivolities.

The pure White woman's desexualization, Moslener tells us, was designed to infer White moral superiority. In short, she was doing PR—whitewashing her husband's and her nation's sins, including genocide and slavery. At the same time, it gave White women the chance not to be someone powerful exactly but to be *adjacent* to someone powerful. As I describe it above, the number 2 to his number 1. Soft, silent, sweet, and *so close to the top*. Just as it does in purity culture today.

Moslener continues to steep us in history—taking us to the twentieth century, when the Pure White Woman emblem was used to separate Black from White at a time when only "free White persons" were awarded citizenship. She details the horrific lynching of countless Black men accused of raping White women, and the lies many of these women told to maintain the myth of innocence awarded to pure White womanhood. And on and on she goes, all the way to modern times, walking us through ways in which the fantasy of the Pure White Woman continues to maintain racial inequality, inequity, and injustice today.

Yet perhaps the most groundbreaking aspect of Moslener's book is her explanation of how purity culture's obligatory disembodiment makes all this *invisible*.

Moslener defines embodiment as the lived experience of the body. This includes physical sensation, the experience of movement, and emotion. But it also includes our ability to sense, feel, and *be* in the world. That is, to be present to *this* time, *this* place, *these* circumstances. Finally, it allows us to engage the ways in which our bodies situate us in society, and how that shapes our subjective sense and experience of life.

To say that these elements of embodiment are discouraged in purity culture is a vast understatement. The church teaches that this kind of body-involvement is nonspiritual, selfish, dangerous, even sinful. *Dis*embodiment, on the other hand—which Moslener defines as "the cognitive state that devalues or dismisses the lived experience of the body"—is framed as a "sacrament" and "lauded as a virtue."

Evangelicalism's anti-embodiment mentality can be seen in its extreme form of abstinence-only-before-marriage messaging, its highly spiritualized diet culture, hunger fasts, faith-healings, and—as Moslener extensively illustrates in this book—its color-evasive theology, which ignores racial difference, as well racial inequity and the systems that perpetuate it.

High-control religious subcultures like White, American, evangelical Christianity *thrive* on congregational disembodiment, as disembodiment prevents congregants from seeing systems designed to stifle or control them and others. What's more, it creates a state of passive dependence upon religious leadership. Taught that our bodies and perceptions are earthly at best and evil at worst, many evangelicals master the suppression of genuine bodily experience, relying on religious leaders to tell them the *right* thing to think, feel, and do. As a result, *re*-embodiment is one of the most vital projects of purity culture recovery.

Many frame recovery in two parts: deconstruction and reconstruction. In deconstruction, we notice, we evaluate and choose to accept or reject our current cognitive and behavioral habits. In reconstruction, we connect to ourselves and develop the capacity to experience and assess the world on our own terms. For many, this includes wrestling with issues of gender, sexuality, race, racism, and colonialism.

Unfortunately, most White folks come to the latter issues on this list later. I certainly did.

Due to our delay, people of color can be retraumatized within purity culture recovery spaces, which tend to be predominantly White. Though some people of color find solidarity around issues of sex and gender, too many tell me that the silence around racism and colonialism leaves them feeling more invisible and alone than when they arrived.

It is imperative for the field of purity culture studies to address the intersectionality of oppression, as well as the overwhelming Whiteness of the voices and stories that dominate our field—including those shared in my own book—and the results of that homogeneity.

In examining the relationship between purity culture and White supremacy, Moslener takes on this urgently needed task. And in doing so, she gives us the opportunity to be *re*-embodied in place and time—connecting us to our pasts, to our present, and to the ways in which we have shaped, and been shaped by, one another.

As you read this book, I urge you to remain connected to your body. If you were raised in purity culture, it may be difficult. That's okay. Notice when you disengage. Pay attention to when you feel angry, defensive, or sad. Notice the guilt, if it arises, and when it turns into shame. Observe when your heart rate increases or you start to have intrusive thoughts. And when you need it, tend to your body. Take a break. Place a supportive hand on the part of you that is reacting strongly. Or hop on the highway and scream.

But stay with it. Feel it. Be in the discomfort, if only for a moment, before you let it go.

This is the way forward.

—LINDA KAY KLEIN

AFTER
PURITY

PURE IN AMERICA

FOR AN EVANGELICAL TEENAGER in the late 1980s, a school trip to Washington, DC, was not so much a field trip to study the democratic process through its museums, memorials, and archives as it was an effort to reclaim America for God. With a busload of classmates from my Christian school, I traveled to the US capital every January 22 to protest the forces that allowed women to prioritize their own well-being over that of their unborn children. The March for Life, of the national pro-life movement, allowed me to flex the muscles of my newly budding Christian womanhood. I was enthralled by the opportunity to be part of something big and important, and attending the march effectively diverted my attention away from the larger, more complicated questions my teenage brain had not yet had the opportunity to consider.

In those years I stood on the lawn of the National Mall, straining to hear political and religious leaders decry the moral failings of a nation, getting high on my own self-righteousness. I was fourteen when I first attended the March for Life. I knew nothing about the dilemmas faced by women who consider and select abortion. But I did know, without a doubt, that as a Christian my way of living and believing was best, not just for me but for everyone. No doubt there were varying degrees of commitment to the cause on those school trips, but I was all in.

By my senior year in college, I had already started dismantling the religious lessons of my youth. When I was hired to work at a local church event, I learned just how much was already falling away. The event was sponsored by an organization I had never heard of, True Love Waits, and was held at the kind of church that required its own technical support staff, leaving me free to observe and reflect on my own evangelical adolescence. The purpose of this event was to encourage young people to take a pledge for sexual abstinence, but it also had an explicitly pro-life message. Anti-abortion activist Gianna Jessen presented her testimony in which she described her mother's experience as a pregnant adolescent who attempted to abort her child. The abortion failed, according to the testimony, and the child was rescued by a nurse at the hospital. This child, the evening's speaker, was now an adult with a slight physical disability who used her early childhood experience to warn contemporary adolescents about the dire consequences and complexities of premarital sex. Afterward, Jessen invited the audience of junior high school students to come forward to sign the True Love Waits pledge, crafted by youth ministers in the Southern Baptist Convention (SBC), a Christian denomination.

In the 1980s, the SBC began developing a sexual education program when conservative evangelicals lost trust in Surgeon General C. Everett Koop, who declined to promote abstinence-only education. Koop encouraged evangelical and other conservative churches to design their own sexual education programs shaped by their religious teachings, but for public educational purposes Koop remained an advocate of comprehensive sex education. Increasingly on the defensive, SBC leaders disparaged gay men and their allies who struggled to raise awareness about HIV/AIDS. Most famously the Reverend Jerry Falwell used the crisis to preach polemics against a so-called gay lifestyle, calling AIDS God's punishment for the sin of homosexuality.[1] In 1987 the first panels of the AIDS Memorial Quilt were displayed on the lawn of the National Mall, each panel dedicated to a victim of the virus.

The SBC continued its anti-gay agenda into the 1990s, when it issued a warning shot in the quickly escalating culture wars and what it perceived to be an assault on their religious freedom. Their target was the American Broadcasting Corporation and its parent company, Disney, whom conservative evangelicals accused of defiling the sacred institution of the family by hosting same-sex family days at its theme park. When Ellen DeGeneres came out as gay on her ABC sitcom in 1997, the SBC had had enough and threatened a boycott of the network that proved the largest evangelical organization in the US was well-equipped for a confrontation with Disney.

At the same time, Richard Ross was a youth minister at Tulip Grove Baptist Church in Old Hickory, Tennessee. Heeding the call from C. Everett Koop, Ross designed a youth group curriculum teaching abstinence-only education, one that was attached to ambitions for national transformation. Ross, now a professor of youth ministers at Southwestern Baptist Theological Seminary, recently reminisced with Scott McDowell, the son of Josh McDowell, an early advocate of sexual purity. Following his father, McDowell celebrated Ross's work and asked about its early days.[2] Ross described how members of his youth group in early 1992 noted the increased presence and support for LGBTQ youth who were coming out. So he gave them a charge: "Well, why don't *you* come out of the closet?" Two years later, True Love Waits hit the national scene with an immense display of over two hundred thousand signed purity pledge cards deposited on the lawn of the National Mall. Printed on each card was the True Love Waits pledge:

> Believing that True Love Waits, I make a commitment to God, myself, my family, my friends, my future mate, and my future children to be sexually abstinent from this day until the day I enter biblical marriage relationship.[3]

Media coverage was extensive. The *Washington Post* declared a "new chapter in the sexual revolution," and the *New York Times* quoted teenage pledgers encouraging virgins to "come out of the closet."[4] It was nothing less than a phenomenon, as young people signed cards and sent them to be counted and displayed in the Georgia Dome, on the Golden Gate Bridge, and SBC convention meetings. Even Disney joined in, promoting their young stars as exemplars of sexual abstinence. Britney Spears, the Jonas Brothers, Miley Cyrus, and countless other young artists who began their careers with Disney sported and spoke about the rings they wore to signify sexual purity. By the early 2000s, purity rings and public declarations of abstinence before marriage were a regular feature of American youth culture.[5]

In her book *Sex and the Soul: Juggling Spirituality, Sexuality, Romance, and Religion on America's College Campuses*, Donna Freitas coined the term *evangelical purity culture* to describe the unique set of dynamics she observed at evangelical colleges.[6] Steeped in romantic mythologies and the rhetoric of sexual danger, evangelical purity culture identified not just a movement but also a cultural shift that positioned evangelical teenagers and their sexual decision-making squarely within evangelical political ambitions. Decades later, many of those former adolescents are also former evangelicals, having left the faith tradition of their youth, recognizing how their youthful desires for love and security were exploited by the political ambitions of church leaders.

For many years I have dedicated my work to listening to stories about the problems caused by evangelical purity culture. In 2019, I conceived of the After Purity Project to formalize this work. I've listened to people talk about their experiences growing up evangelical and the problems that persist with navigating early lessons of sexual fear and with trusting religious authority after the need for approval turned abusive. Each and every story was familiar to me. I was open with my research participants, noting that I, too, had been shaped by these same forces. Even as an academic who has studied purity culture for almost twenty years, I continue to struggle with its aftermath, searching for habits of meaning-making that are not in conflict with my lived and embodied experiences.

In her book *Against Purity: Living Ethically in Compromised Times*, social and political theorist Alexis Shotwell interrogates this desire for purity, pointing toward the ways that human beings are already and always have been implicated and contaminated by the pollutants we seek to protect ourselves from. Efforts to seek and obtain purity, Shotwell explains, deny the ways we are formed in connection to one another and to our pasts, cultivating illusions of individual and collective innocence. Among White people, cultivating purity and innocence creates a *dilemma of disembodiment* where "ignorance, repression, and active disavowal" encourage practices of historical amnesia.[7] Myths of innocence cannot withstand historical truth-telling.

The problem with purity isn't about the desire to be good or feel safe. The problem with purity is that it creates the illusion that you must be good in order to be deserving of love and security. In order to preserve this illusion we have learned to perpetrate a number of falsehoods about ourselves, our sexualities, our gender conditioning, our racial identities, and our collective histories. We've learned to distort truth and market a false optimism invested in myths of our own innocence.

When a crisis of purity erupts, around adolescent sexuality or national identity, innocence demands a return to something that *signals* a presumed source of truth, virtue, and safety, doubling down on the illusion that the status quo offers just that. Among former evangelicals raised to embody the virtue of sexual purity, resisting the privileges ascribed to White, Christian citizenship requires dismantling many of the myths used to preserve the beliefs that the USA is once and always destined for greatness. Since 2016 and the first election of Donald Trump, many White evangelicals have come to realize that greatness is often far from goodness. What was already a slow exodus has since become a thunderous retreat from Christian denominations and churches that had grown used to their religious claims engendering political influence. For the people departing these institutions this often means separation from or conflict with families, close-knit communities, and belief systems that are invested in and tangibly benefit from the tenets of White Christian nationalism. For those who leave, it has meant recognizing how theological orthodoxy among White Christians is born of the same tree that produces the strange fruit of racial and sexual violence.

Since the early 1990s, evangelical adolescents have been recruited into the myth-making of Christian America, to live as exemplars for a nation and for its churches unable to reckon with the fact of human bodies. Christian purity campaigns were designed to promote the myth of national innocence. By positioning sexually pure teenagers as emblems of national prosperity and security, organizations like the Southern Baptist Convention have demonstrated a continued investment in national myths that exonerate us from our collective past. Seeking purity, evangelical leaders and their political allies have taught White youth to believe their innocence is a projection of our nation's past. Historical white-washing is the common term, where histories of genocide, slavery, and other immoral acts perpetrated by European settler-colonists are transformed into spiritualized myths that celebrate God's sovereignty and blessing upon the creation of a new nation-state.

Long before adolescence became a category of human development and a site of civilizational promise, nation-building projects of the nineteenth century regarded White women as progenitors of national greatness. Reversing almost two centuries of Christian theology that regarded women as morally, spiritually, and physically inferior, nineteenth-century gender ideologies popularized among American Protestants constructed a White racial ideal bound up with the reproductive and alleged civilizing capacity of "true" womanhood. Efforts toward White women's full political enfranchisement benefited from this shift, with prominent women leaning heavily on their own presumed virtues to argue for increased political enfranchisement.

Often, these arguments were made at the expense of people of color, whose humanity was further devalued as White women's representational status increased. In my book *Virgin Nation: Sexual Purity and American Adolescence*, I argue that sexual purity as practice and rhetoric has been utilized by White Protestant evangelicals to secure and maintain their own political dominance. As such, sexual purity has been a tool for building a White, Christian America, with White womanhood serving as both beacon and boundary for its creation.

In the nineteenth century, White Protestants established a nationalistic narrative asserting that the fate of the United States as a geopolitical and economic power rested on the iconic symbolism of White women's ability to birth and nurture a great civilization. A particularly telling embodiment is portrayed in John Gast's allegorical 1872 painting *American Progress*, in which national growth and vitality is embodied by White womanhood. Created for a travel brochure advertising the American West, Gast's painting depicts a White woman, the allegorical Columbia, holding a schoolbook and laying telegraph wire as she floats westward in attire that could be seen as either angelic or neoclassical. The sky ahead of her is dark and cloudy, and the group of Indigenous people and untamed animals are forced to cower in her blinding presence. Behind her, the clear horizon illuminates an eastern coastline bustling with commerce, while beneath her, enlightened by her presence, are White men with domesticated animals ready to plow the land and reap its harvest.

Gast's *American Progress* would become synonymous with the doctrine of Manifest Destiny, an ideology purporting that White settlers were entitled to land expansion without regard for the bodies of the inhabitants already present. Manifest Destiny extolled a sexually pure White womanhood that obscured numerous forms of racialized violence perpetuated against enslaved Africans, Indigenous peoples, and other non-Europeans and non-Christians. The mythic innocence of White womanhood functioned as a nationalistic trope that White women could and did choose to embrace for the benefit of their sex, their race, and their nation. Of course, this protected status could only be maintained by excluding non-White women from this symbolic position.

In *After Purity*, I investigate the myths that perpetuate illusions of innocence about bodies, White racial identity, and national greatness. Each of these necessitate the practice of disembodiment, a cognitive state that devalues or dismisses the lived experience of the body and how our bodies situate us within systems of privilege and oppression. For people who grew up in and out of purity culture, this has meant struggling to accept and learn from sexual and other bodily desires. It has meant extended periods of recovery from gender-based and sexual violence. For White people, it has meant being socialized into color-evasive ideologies about race and then struggling to understand or even disdaining claims about the systemic nature of racial inequality. In both cases, ignoring the body is mistakenly lauded as a virtue. Denying the sexual prompts of one's body has often been a sign of holiness in the Christian faith tradition. Likewise, claiming to "not see race" is presumed to be a virtuous stance regarding racial difference. In both cases these disembodied practices perform significant violence, as erasure of bodies and their needs means developing cognitive habits that refuse to see harm if it conflicts with our established innocence myths.

I began this book as an interview study, the After Purity Project. Using social media, I advertised for research participants willing to share their experiences of growing up and out of purity culture. I began cultivating an online presence as the After Purity Project and discovered a robust community of people already building networks based on shared experiences within White evangelicalism. Today there are numerous projects, academic and autobiographical, seeking to make sense of an era when White evangelical ascendancy excited many young people and helped us feel important and loved. The ensuing crush of these illusions was a frequent theme of my interviews. Finding people to share their stories required little effort. In part because of social media but also because of the collective need of former evangelicals to make sense out of their own spiritual, racial, and gender formation. Their stories are the foundation of this book. Their stories are the reason why I am able to include parts of my own. I did not make this decision lightly or quickly. But when I realized that disembodiment was a major theme of my interviews, I knew that I could not rely on the traditional academic voice of the invisible expert.

In this book, I include my own stories alongside those of my research participants because one goal of this project is to situate our adolescent experiences within broader histories of the denominations and political movements that shape us. Referencing my own experiences helps illuminate the ways that our gender, sexual, and racial identities were informed by forces beyond our comprehension. Despite our national insistence on individualism, we need to understand how our ability to make meaning is controlled by a set of collective myths. *After Purity* is a book about these myths, in which you will see me demythologize my White, evangelical childhood and adolescence. I hope it helps you do the same.

The stories of the sixty-five people I interviewed illuminate a great deal about our collective need for safety and innocence when situated within broader histories of evangelical Christianity and US political life. The immediate context for these stories comprises the two major reckonings around race and sexuality that have recently cracked the illusions of our national myths: the MeToo movement and Black Lives Matter. MeToo revealed how widespread the problems of sexual exploitation, gender-based violence, and sexual assault remain within every US institution. It split open cracks in our religious institutions to reveal how deeply invested evangelical Protestants are in protecting the veracity of their own theological claims—including the work of the Southern Baptist Convention, the same institution that has led the evangelical purity movement since the early 1990s, which denies and dismisses survivors' claims of sexual assault within its own churches.

Black Lives Matter surged from national to international promi-nence as the crisis of police brutality created new demands for ac-countability around histories of racism and White supremacy in the nation. Among religious and political conservatives, resistance to accountability around both of these topics was framed as an issue of child protection and parental rights: currently eighteen states have laws based in the fear that children are being corrupted by how public schools teach US history and human sexuality. As for the Southern Baptists in particular, conversations about racism and White suprem-acy are regarded much like the claims of survivors of sexual assault demanding accountability. They are perceived as divisive and demonic threats, incompatible with "biblical" teachings.

The first three chapters of this book begin the demythologizing work the After Purity Project is dedicated to. Participants' stories and meaning-making work launch this inquiry in chapter 1 by detailing the impacts of romantic mythologies and body-denying theologies of evangelical purity culture. Among these are stories of abuse within White evangelical families and institutions, which are the focus of chapter 2. For many years I saw little indication of the extent to which purity culture created an abusive climate within White evangeli-cal communities. I was certainly able to point to harmful teachings rooted in gender stereotypes and sexual fear, but the impact of those teachings was never clear to me, with many women claiming to thrive in their conservative communities. Over the last few years this has shifted dramatically as survivors of sexual assault and gender-based violence have come forward in droves, revealing how purity teach-ings were enforced in response to accusations of sexual misconduct, experiences that have left survivors and their advocates reeling with disillusionment and anger.

Every participant in the After Purity Project is a former evangeli-cal, having left their churches for other churches or faith traditions. During my interviews, I asked each person, "How would you describe your current spiritual or religious commitment?" The varieties and combinations of the answers I received are the focus of chapter 3. Each demonstrates that former evangelicals remain deeply tied to understanding their lives and the world around them as sacred and are seeking new ways to inhabit their beliefs and commitments with integrity.

In these first three chapters, the experiences of White women are overrepresented, a reflection of my research participant pool. In some ways this is a correct representation of the aftermath purity culture, as White women were and are the primary target of recruitment for these campaigns. But as a result our stories have crowded out others, taking up needed space for discussing the intersections of purity and race, a task that requires speaking to our collective failure to engage with our national past. White racial superiority is one of many innocence myths embedded in evangelical purity culture, its tenets remaining unquestioned because the myth of White racial superiority has yet to be acknowledged and understood by many White people as both tangible and capable of harm. The demythologizing work of *After Purity* requires White readers to engage with our racial pasts, both individual and collective.

Chapters 4, 5, and 6 present the history of White supremacy in relation to sexual purity in the United States. Many familiar with evangelical purity culture mark its origins in the late twentieth century. But the virtue of sexual purity was crafted in the nineteenth century as a unique feature of White womanhood. Sexual purity as a virtue for White American women was formed within the Black-White racial binary, constructed first by the institution of slavery and anti-miscegenation laws and reinforced by Jim Crow segregation and the practice of racial-terror lynchings. White women's sexual purity was a weapon of racial superiority refined by White, middle-class Protestants who benefited from assumptions about their own moral character. It was also a shield for White men, who were permitted to behave like sexual monsters toward all other women, exploiting and assaulting the bodies of Black women while using the presumed sexual innocence of White women to exonerate their behavior.

The dominant innocence myth in this book has circulated for generations, one that elevates White womanhood to an emblem of American prosperity and security. Evangelical purity culture of the late 1990s refurbished nineteenth-century practices of US nation building that represent White womanhood as always innocent. Purity culture was one of the many tools that allowed White evangelicals to usher in a new era of White Christian nationalism (WCN). Though newly named by scholars, WCN's political myths, rhetoric, and ideologies are easily spotted in any competent survey of US history. An innocence myth that many accept as part of traditional or "biblical" Christian teaching, the framework of WCN allows us to interrogate the claim that America is a Christian nation, in a special relationship with the Christian God, a tactic used by religious and social conservatives to enact violence against groups that threaten their political and social power. With shifts toward increasing acceptance of queer people as equal citizens and as Christian believers, hard-liners have doubled down on innocence myths, deploying children's vulnerability to justify the dehumanization of gender and sexual minorities who have only just begun to see a collective future. Likewise, the retracting of reproductive freedoms points toward a radical conservative fringe that continues to invest in innocence myths around motherhood, using the symbol of fetuses to decry a nation that has not maintained its close relationship to God. White women, adolescents, children, and the unborn have all played starring roles in the innocence myths of White Christian America. Each has had their time on the national stage to assert claims of innocence about America writ large.

On January 6, 2021, White women were among the throngs who battered their way into the US Capitol. With smeared eye makeup, bullhorns, and cries of "Why us?" when Capitol Police responded with force. White women turned on the nation's capital and its democratic processes by insisting that the election had been stolen from their president-messiah. Reports during and after the violent episode showed how White women's participation was used by the Right to exonerate all participants from legal and moral culpability. The death of Ashli Babbitt elevated the innocence myth of White womanhood to national martyrdom. The women of January 6 proclaimed their innocence, and when documentary evidence contradicted, they pleaded ignorance. In court, they were defended as mothers and wives, their lawyers representing them in the context of their relationships to those who depended on their caregiving work. Over and over, the courts heard that White women whose feminine traits were bolstered by their racial innocence could not possibly be responsible for attacking the capital of a nation whose own innocence myths created those of White womanhood.

The work of *After Purity* is unraveling mythologies of innocence, both personal and collective, that infect our ability to see the United States and its religious institutions in all their sordid truth. Evangelical purity culture is just one of many efforts throughout the history of the United States to reinforce the innocence myths that function at all levels of social organizing: the individual, the family, the church, the nation. Without these myths and their continuous reinforcement, the nation and its residents are left with a past stripped of any pretense toward greatness, displaying the deep wounds and fissures we've been so well trained to ignore. In the present, our Christian churches are left with hollow theologies and empty pews, unable to address widespread crises in religious trauma and sexual abuse. Dismantling the illusions of purity, Whiteness, and Christian supremacy is a disaster for those invested in being great. For the rest of us, it's a moment to awaken, if we haven't yet.

CHAPTER ONE

THE PURITY MYTH

A s a teenager in the 1980s and early '90s, I did not encounter the crushing wave of evangelical purity culture that many of my interviewees described. I experienced more of a gently aggressive tide that lapped at my desire to be and be seen as good. Though being a sexually active teen was always far from my own high school ambitions, I very much enjoyed the status of having a boyfriend. I learned how to perform modesty, which was well-suited to my degree of embarrassment around the finer points of sexual arousal. I learned that boys were tightly wound sexual beasts whose unbridled passion could be released by a hair trigger, a teaching meant to make me afraid but that just made me more curious. What could I do to unlock the savage beast within? What was I *willing* to do? Mind you, at this age I was also completely unable to comprehend the concept of genitalia and fluids, so all my strategizing was strictly "above the equator." I wasn't ready for a sexual relationship, but what I wanted was the status marker that comes with a heterosexual romantic partnership.

In my White evangelical world, marriage and motherhood were status markers for young women to aspire to. The ability to acquire a good Christian boyfriend was about showing one's preparedness for these tasks. What I refer to as evangelical purity culture has an institutional history, one that didn't fully take root in US culture until I was out of high school. However, the tenants of my world were directly informed by the pro-life movement, which elevated marriage and motherhood to sacred status and devalued women who did not pursue these goals.

In 2019, when I started interviewing people who grew up in and eventually out of purity culture, I was interested in gathering data that would provide deeper insight into evangelical purity culture, a nomenclature that had caught on so well that I never once had to explain it. I began my interviews by asking, "How would you describe evangelical purity culture to someone unfamiliar with it?" Though I've spent over fifteen years studying evangelicalism and sexuality in the United States, I wanted to understand how other people at various degrees of separation from the faith of their youth made sense of it for themselves. I found that the answers to my question followed an unsurprising formula, reflecting the hard-line, straightforward messaging of purity teachings. Overwhelming, my respondents (mostly White, mostly women) spoke about learning that a lack of interest in sex and/or active resistance to their own sexual curiosity was essential to maintaining their Christian piety. Their adolescent religious education was dominated by both overt and covert lessons on how to control their bodies.

Embracing the purity myth is both necessary and rewarded for young women who are socialized into religious subcultures that link their worth and value to their readiness for marriage and motherhood. In the Church of Jesus Christ of Latter-day Saints, when young people have maintained a sufficient level of moral piety, their reward is to be deemed "temple ready": they can be admitted into the temple for sacred rights. Among evangelicals, the gatekeeping is less ritualized but no less pronounced, as young people learn to police themselves and one another as they jockey for approval from their religious leaders and parents. Even if personal salvation isn't at risk, the threat of social disgrace and a laundry list of physical, spiritual, and emotional consequences are used to cudgel young people into accepting a narrow understanding of human sexuality.

Time and time again, my respondents echoed what Linda Kay Klein describes in her book *Pure: Inside the Evangelical Movement That Shamed a Generation of Young Women and How I Broke Free.* Sexual purity for young women was an opportunity to demonstrate their Christian devotion. "It's the story of me—a sixteen-year-old girl in her first real relationship. Willing, no wanting, to be tested so she could prove to her God, her community, and *herself* that she was good."[1] The desire to be good and perceived as good is a foundational concept for understanding how purity culture contributes to the powerful symbolism of White womanhood.

Growing up in purity culture meant learning to control our bodies, our desires, and our thoughts as we learned to police ourselves and one another. Implicit in these control measures was a socialization process that trained young people's desire in particular ways, most notably toward the opposite sex in the hope of ensuring that a young person experiencing same-sex desire would be shifted toward heteronormativity. These teachings were overwhelmingly targeted at young women, with lessons about sexual danger, potential self-hatred, and double-standards, including an overwhelming emphasis on the belief that young women's bodies and behavior have the power to control the thoughts and actions of boys and men.

My own story resonates deeply with my research participants in our shared need to be and be seen as good, making us deserving of protection from sexual danger. I began learning this lesson at the age of six when my first-grade teacher at the small Christian school I attended pulled my friend Michelle and me into the hallway. She had us sit with her on the worn marble steps leading upstairs to the older grades while she explained that we had done something wrong. I don't recall her words, but I recall the humiliation of being pulled out of class to be reprimanded. Michelle and I had let boys see our underwear. I had been in the cloak room, standing with my legs spread between a shelf and the coat rack, letting them look under my dress. Miss Marshall may have said something to us about how to properly behave when wearing a dress, about keeping parts of our body hidden, about boys and their curiosity. Her particular lessons are lost to memory, but for decades the memory of that cloakroom carried deep shame for me.

This memory became a narrative about myself that I've carried around my entire life. By the age of six I craved attention from boys. I was willing to exploit my body to get it. The cloakroom was not the only site of boy-crazy behavior. During recess, I would play a game with a fifth grader named Travis. Our school basement was a brown concrete box, the walls lined with thick athletic mats that were used during gym class and kept the more rambunctious kids from a skull-cracking collision. I was especially captivated by Travis, his lack of fear and freedom of movement. While he played basketball in the school basement with other boys, I would hide away like a kidnapped princess. I'd wait for a pause in his game and then scream, "Travis! Come save me!" My hero would exit the court and race toward me, pick me up from my invisible prison, and carry me to the safety of the small, steel jungle gym, the one place in the basement where I learned to indulge my own physical dexterity. When I got tired of the exertion, I could count on Travis to help me exercise my creativity and take me to a less brown, less concrete world where I was important enough to have my fictional requests for salvation taken seriously.

For decades these memories haunted me, as if they indicated a deep-seated need for a male companion and savior. Without realizing it, the scriptures I was required to memorize in school began filling in the spaces that were left hollow with shame. They fit nicely. In the story of the Garden of Eden, Eve's punishment from God is not the same at Adam's. "Your desire will be for your husband and he will rule over you." (Genesis 3:16) Sin had entered the world, and the paradise of mutual relations between men and women was lost. For women, the loss was greater, a point that the Apostle Paul would later amplify in the New Testament to argue that women are spiritually inferior, emotionally incomplete, and a collective nuisance in need of regular reminders to be silent. For me this meant a life of depending on men for various forms of personal fulfillment, a romantic relationship leading to marriage the mark of my success. I would live by the curse, obey where Eve disobeyed, and be rewarded with a man to care for and to protect me.

Shame does powerful work with our memories. I was a bad princess who had to demand attention from boys and at the age of six was willing to perform for male sexual curiosity to gain that attention. But sometimes the veil of shame is lifted, and in this case it was thanks to my experimentation with cannabis that moved me beyond the limits of my sober, adult imagination. I'm an infrequent user, because sometimes memories emerge that I do not yet have the emotional capacity to handle. And sometimes they emerge with such unprecedented clarity that I have to pay attention.

One evening, after a day of writing, I was prepared to leave my memories to rest. Dinner and a smoke were wooing me into a pleasant evening when I began not just to see but to feel that cloakroom. A muscle memory was emerging from a hidden storage unit in my body. My six-year-old legs were climbing a shelf, leading to a daring lunge to bridge the gap between the shelf and a bar of the coat rack. I stood with arms and legs spread wide, feeling large and powerful. And then I jumped, arms in, legs in. To the ground. Then I started climbing up to do it all over again. I did this with my friend Michelle. We'd face each other because it gave us courage, the synchronicity of our movements emboldening our bodies. It was during this gymnastic feat that the boys entered the cloakroom, peeking around the door with curiosity and a little bit of envy. Again, we jumped to the floor, proud of our newly discovered skill.

I've held two versions of this story in my body for decades, but only one was audible to me. The revelation that I wasn't a six-year-old who craved sexual attention from boys was baffling, not because it was inconsistent with who I knew myself to be but because that narrative had been deeply lodged in my hippocampus for so long. At the age of forty-nine my body finally surfaced the second version of this story, confirming its veracity in the release of shame that accompanied it. I'd been studying purity culture for over fifteen years, was actively working on my second book on the topic, only then to discover the seeds of my sexual shame uprooted by a physical memory of my childhood body being strong, adventurous, and at play.

I learned that day on those steps that my body held secrets I didn't yet understand, secrets that boys were desperate to know. This fear followed me for decades, complicating my feelings of sexual desire and encouraging me to build a fortress whose centurions diligently patrolled for sexual danger. The false memory remains in my body, influencing my choices and behavior, even as a more true version has surfaced. This is something I heard over and over again from my research participants: you can choose to leave purity culture behind, but not your body. Hidden beneath layers of forgotten memories, lessons of sexual fear and shame have continued to emit these same messages to our bodies even after our break from purity culture. Our bodies have been trained to practice purity as a form Christian piety.

Because White evangelicalism has few external indicators of faith commitments beyond one's personal behavior and physical expression, religious piety is often expressed in a mash-up of the sacred and secular. My own princess rescue ritual was an amalgamation of romantic mythologies and Eve's curse. Evangelical purity culture offered a tangible set of practices for performing piety. For many of us, purity was fundamental to our adolescent Christian faith, as we learned that the salvation of our souls depended on relinquishing our bodily desires.

Though only a handful of men participated in the After Purity research project, two of them discussed learning that Christian piety required them to control their sexual behavior. Brian, who would later become a youth minister, remembers being taught that "no sex before marriage" came straight from the synoptic gospels, the set of biblical texts that focus on the teachings of Jesus. However, in evangelical circles, the concept of the "gospel" is used more broadly to refer to mandates that are inferred from the teachings of Jesus. Most of the biblical Christian texts regarding sex and gender are attributed not to Jesus but to the Apostle Paul, who wrote prolifically (and problematically) about women's roles in the church and the need to control sexuality. None of Paul's writings appear in what biblical scholars refer to as the Gospels since he was not a contemporary of Jesus. Regardless, Brian's adolescent faith was deeply informed by the belief that in order for him to be regarded as a faithful follower of Christ, he needed to resist any desire to engage in sexual activity prior to marriage.[2]

For Will, this same mandate meant that his adolescent sexuality was formed through a cycle of resistance, temptation, and repentance.

> And so it would be, you know, two teenage Christians that would be trying to do the right thing and not be sexually active, but then we would fall and then we'd repent and we would say, okay, never again. And then we would do it again. And it was just a constant cycle of back and forth. So that was a lot of that resisting. It was like a constant struggle if you will, and constantly fighting that.[3]

Later in our interview, Will described how these early patterns infiltrated his first marriage. The habit of connecting shame with acting on his sexual desire did not end when he entered marriage, which he did just out of college. He described feeling an immense amount of pressure to marry because of a natural desire for sex that could not be expressed outside of a marriage relationship. Like many young people, Will was also fed a steady diet of unrealistic expectations about married sex, which has been described by purity advocates as a release of pent-up pleasure possible at any given moment.

Silver Ring Thing, a purity ministry whose events I attended early in my research, emphasizes the reward of married sex. At one event, a newly married evangelist for the group described his wedding ring as "an all-day ride pass," eliciting whoops and cheers from the teen audience and even led them in chants of "sex is great!" followed by the caveat that this is so only in the context of marriage. These heightened expectations for marital sex are necessary for convincing young people that waiting for sex will be rewarded with the best sex ever. For Will, going into marriage with the weight of shame and the pressure of expectations took a significant toll on his relationship. And though he acknowledges that many factors led to his divorce, the sexual frustration and expectations he carried with him played a significant part in the failure of his marriage.

Christian piety is often articulated as a relationship: "it's not a religion; it's a relationship" is an evangelical tag that attempts to distinguish Christianity as somehow set aside for the serious believer. Young people learned that abstaining from sex was essential to maintaining this relationship. As Nicole, an After Purity Project participant, explained to me, "It's not just me making an active decision not to have sex. It's me making an active decision to, like, have a relationship with God, have a relationship with my church, be that kind of person in my community. It's so further reaching than just my body and my choices."[4]

Purity teachings impressed upon Nicole the importance of preparing for and staying in relationship with God and her community, which would prepare her to enter the ultimate relationship: Christian marriage. These teachings incorporated a series of behaviors and practices, labeled as Christian morality, that required her to make ultimate meaning out of the promise of one day entering into a biblical marriage. Nicole explained this in our interview:

> God commanded that a man and a woman stay pure and stay connected to one another, and God has a person out there for you who is for you only, for you and your duty as a woman and as a Christian is to keep yourself pure before you meet that person. So

that when you are with that person, you are only sharing yourself with them because that's what God commands. It's a lifestyle. It's not a choice. It's the question of your life, of your soul, of your, you know, of everything about you, and it's just all consuming.

Rebecca, another After Purity Project participant, also learned that sexual restraint was about maintaining a relationship with God. She referred to it as a "drumbeat" evoking the discipline and control required to practice this particular form of religious piety.[5] Likewise, Duncan, a former youth minister, taught students to approach dating as a godly friendship that should not be entered into unless both partners did so with a primary focus on their relationship to God.[6] Angela learned that "saving herself for marriage" was a form of holiness, a spiritual form of boundary marking that allowed her to be reassured of eternal salvation. It's not accidental that salvific language is used by purity advocates, who also characterize marriage and sex within marriage as an eternal reward for obedience. While Angela learned to distinguish between holiness and impurity by maintaining her physical and sexual boundaries, she also learned that her sexuality was a threat to the fate of her soul. To disobey those boundaries threatened her holiness and would leave her spiritually blemished.[7]

Shelly, another participant, explained that purity culture taught her to regulate her body in hopes of being found without fault. As a woman this was the greatest value she could achieve. She noted that these mandates controlled her thoughts and interactions within both her opposite-sex and same-sex relationships, presumably because of concerns that she may become overly attached to other girls. Shelly learned to self-regulate so that the self she projected into the world would reflect the virtue of modesty that reflected well on her community.[8]

Evangelical purity culture deploys boundary markers around gender and sexuality in order to activate the in-group/out-group dynamics evangelicals believe are necessary for maintaining the distinct nature of their collective identity—what they refer to as "being in but not of the world." Like many evangelical adolescents, Angela learned that her personal holiness was not simply a matter of personal salvation but about reassuring her entire community that it existed within a true and secure faith system whose promises of marital happiness and eternal salvation were real.

In later chapters I will demonstrate how these sexual and gender boundaries parallel the same dynamics around racial boundaries in order to replicate racial hierarchies and reinforce racialized, sexual stereotypes, including the myth of White women's sexual innocence. But it's important to note that the vast majority of my White interviewees never mentioned the racist assumptions of sexual purity because they had learned to unsee race, including their own racial identity.

The boundaries around sex and gender within White evangelicalism are presented as biblical mandates. Beginning in the 1970s organizations such as the Focus on the Family and the Council on Biblical Manhood and Womanhood (CBMW) mistakenly (or not) promoted nineteenth-century gender roles as uniquely biblical, offering stern warnings against any deviation. The original logo of Focus on the Family, which still graces the gated entrance of their headquarters in Colorado Springs, presents a nineteenth-century White couple with the husband pictured above his wife, both gazing down at their infant child. Focus on the Family elevated a time period when women were deprived of the right to control their fertility (though the fortunate always found ways to do so), divorce an abusive spouse, hold property, vote, or run for political office. It was also a time period when fears of immigration, race-mixing, and increased rights for formerly enslaved people prompted numerous projects of White racial violence. These included scientific racism, which graded non-Whites as genetically inferior; racial-terror lynchings, used to remind African Americans of their vulnerability to Whites; and legal decisions determining who was White enough to become a citizen of the United States.

James Dobson, founder of Focus on the Family, had been trained by eugenicist Paul Popenoe, who taught him that homosexuality and feminism were threats to family integrity and that the strength of the American family rested in genetic compatibility and gender complementarianism.[9] Dobson was also deeply informed by George Gilder, cofounder of Discovery Institute, which seeks to promote creationism and undermine evolutionary science. Gilder's theory of civilizational expansion asserts a gender/sex binary in which men and women are biologically and psychologically created to be distinct and complementary in their social and biological functions. This design, Gilder and Dobson argue, is a natural order that promotes healthy families, thriving communities, and a stable nation-state. In his book *Men and Marriage*, first published in 1975 under the title *Sexual Suicide*, Gilder claimed that civilizations advance only when men and women properly understand their roles.[10] Men are designed to rule civilization but are innately destructive. In order for their power to be harnessed for the creation and maintenance of civilization, women must use their innate nurturing skills to make marriage and parenting appealing to men. Without the institution of the heteronormative family, men's ruling power becomes destructive and civilization will not advance.[11]

Dobson and groups such as the CBMW and the Southern Baptist Convention anointed this theory as the biblical standard for marriage and family. Today evangelicals still speak incessantly of complementarian gender roles and seek to determine how their lives can more fully conform to this ideal. Evangelical purity culture was shaped around these standards, teaching young people to recognize their distinct gendered nature. Young men are taught that their bodies are capable of harm, their sexual desires are bad, and that their female peers have a power over them they must learn to resist. Interestingly enough, young women are not taught that they have power over men but that they can easily influence or seduce men with their bodies and behavior, a choice that subverts the gendered order.

Given the broader sexual and racial politics of White evangelicalism, it's no surprise that themes of bodily control, including the control of sexual desires, appeared frequently in my interviews.

Participants talked of programming, double-binds, regulations, suppression, rigid sets of rules and monitoring. Evangelical purity culture
is a regime of bodily control that disciplines young bodies into a very
narrow understanding of sexual and gender expression. For many, this
caused deep anxiety and frustration once they began experiencing
sexual desire in their adolescence. For Will, who found himself in a
mad cycle of failure and repentance, adolescence was a daily struggle
to understand how he should respond to his attraction toward girls,
which he learned not to accept as a natural part of his sexual development but as an instinct he needed to suppress. He carefully studied
popular Christian texts like Stephen Arterburn's *Every Man's Battle*,
he told me, in order to "build a fortress around my internal desires."
He described this particular book as filled with mixed messages,
teaching him that while his sexual desires were created by God, they
had to be suppressed because "flesh was of the devil."

Laura, another participant in the After Purity Project, talked to
me about the same rigid set of rules that Will encountered in his
books, but she also noted a litany of *unspoken* rules about how to
interact with people you were attracted to.

For many, the rules of evangelical purity culture did not need to
be written down because they were prescribed as singular truth rooted
in the belief that heteronormative marriage was the only acceptable
form of family. "Everyone's assumed to have the same experience,"
Laura explained. A cisgender women married to a trans man, she
reflected on how the rules of purity culture were written to socialize
young people into heteronormative frameworks. For young people
experiencing gender dysphoria or questioning their gender identity,
the rules of purity culture nullified any attempt to explore other varia-
tions of gender expression.

Youth leaders who teach purity culture draw on an arsenal of
object lessons to demonstrate the stakes of bodily control. Angela
described one of these: "So if you're in evangelical purity culture,
you've probably gone to youth group when you were fifteen, and

you've had a youth pastor take out a candy bar and ask you to pass it around unwrapped and then talk about how that's your body." After being handled by numerous people without its packaging, the candy bar becomes undesirable. Purity teachings emphasize that the value of one's body diminishes with physical encounters and with it the ability of that individual to experience genuine physical pleasure. Other object lessons within purity culture emphasize that numerous physical encounters deplete one's ability to create emotional intimacy, the way a piece of tape loses its ability to stick when used over and over again. The ability to control one's body is an obedience practice that grants people the right to a very narrowly defined but presumably superior form of sexual intimacy.

Will explained how the practice of these teachings ill-prepared him for marriage by setting up impossible expectations. He was taught to believe that "once we were married, everything will be great, and our sex lives would be so fulfilling and wonderful and dynamic." But he found that the habits of purity culture, especially feeling shame around sexual desire, did not disappear in his marriage. The gender dynamics of White evangelicalism, which prioritize male sexual pleasure, made navigating marital sexuality a strain rather than a joyful experience. As his marriage ended, Will understood the full extent of purity culture and how his expectations for marriage remained deeply informed by his earliest lessons about sexuality. Rather than provide him with resources for working through the challenges of his marriage, his evangelical beliefs only reinforced the need for spiritual and relational perfectionism, ideals that he never learned to reconcile with his sexual desire.

Since the 1970s, evangelicals have been very wary of their reputation for being sex-negative and have strategically drawn from elements of the sexual revolution to change this perception. This means that young people at a purity event may be asked to scream, "Sex is great!" at the top of their lungs. But they do so with the understanding that sex is only great within a heterosexual marriage. My interviews suggest, however, that whatever sex-positive messaging purity evangelists may offer, overwhelming themes of sexual shame flourish. Women in particular internalize the belief that sex is an obligation and not meant for their enjoyment. For participant Brook that meant learning about sex from her mother and a chocolate brownie. Rather than explaining that desiring sex is like desiring a chocolate brownie that belongs to someone else, Brook's mom chewed up the brownie and then spit it into her daughter's face. Sex and the desire for it, according to Brook's mother, is a repulsive and demoralizing act that women are not meant to enjoy.

Many of the women I interviewed spoke at length about the ways they were encouraged to dress modestly to signify their ability to control their bodies. During a year she spent at a Christian school, Caroline was required to participate in modesty checks in which all the girls lifted their hands above their heads and then bent over to touch their toes. The revelation of any flesh from the torso or back meant detention and a trip to what Caroline called the "closet of shame," where girls found clothing that met the school's modesty requirements.

The practice of modesty is not unique to evangelicalism, but its meanings vary from community to community. Within the Nation of Islam (NOI), women learn to sew their own garments so they can produce clothes that meet modesty standards that require covering the hair, arms, and legs. However, the fashion produced by members of the Nation of Islam is not required to be demure. In fact, mosques hold their own fashion shows to display the work of Muslim women. Modest fashion has even hit the runway, with Muslim designers finding a place for their work in the mainstream fashion industry. For women in the NOI, modesty may mean covering one's skin and hair, but it does not mean rejecting fashionable or even avant garde trends that display personal style or even wealth. The opposite is true in so-called Plain Communities, where women dress in a way that is designed to demonstrate their separation from the world and reject any desire for worldly goods or wealth. Old World Mennonite,

Amish, and some Quakers wear clothes designed according to old-world standards, more similar to the clothing of eighteenth-century European agrarian communities. Modesty in this context is simplicity of dress, including head coverings, to demonstrate female submission, though showing legs, ankles, arms, and elbows is acceptable.

Most contemporary evangelicals do not exist on the margins of the US religious landscape. Many White evangelicals seek to impart their values and beliefs into the cultural mainstream. Unlike the modesty practices of Plain Communities or the Nation of Islam, evangelical modesty practices are not so pronounced that their clothing announces them as cultural outsiders. It's not surprising then that none of my interviewees described their religious communities as requiring a form of dress that would mark them as outside the mainstream. But that doesn't mean that clothing choices were not monitored and adjudicated as modest or immodest. As Shelly noted above, modesty is not just about her ability to demonstrate her self-control but about how that reflects on her community. For young evangelical women, these choices are first and foremost about being a witness to the secular world, demonstrating a way of being that is presumably superior to all others.

A couple of the women I interviewed spoke about how the intense pressures to control their bodies resulted in eating disorders. Only by controlling their physical appetites could they achieve the mandate to suppress their sexuality while maintaining a degree of sexual availability for attracting a husband. Cynda explained that her evangelical upbringing taught her that her value was inherently tied to her ability to attract and marry a man. But at the same time, she had to control her behavior and appearance so as not to be perceived as sexy. Cynda dealt with the resulting tension in her body by developing an eating disorder. As she explained to me, "Eating disorders are sort of a way out of that double-bind, because you're able to be feminine and prototypically attractive while [you] also desexualize your body."

Cynda wasn't the only respondent who discussed her eating disorder. Anna said that purity culture allowed her to fully detach from all bodily needs, including food and sexual desire. Because of its promotion of mandatory heterosexuality, purity culture provides no room for young people experiencing same-sex attraction to attend to those desires. The only option is to shut down those feelings. Anna became accustomed to this habit, one that eventually translated into an unhealthy relationship with food. She controlled the discomfort she felt in her body from denying her sexuality by projecting those energies into her eating habits, which were equally restrained. In treatment for an eating disorder, Anna was able to heal her relationship both with food and with sexual desire. Shortly after, she came out as gay. Her counselor explained that eating disorders were common among women struggling to acknowledge their sexual identity. Anna's story allows us to understand how purity culture promotes the idea that bodily desires for food and sex are a threat to personal piety. Not to mention that desiring the wrong kind of body is as indicative of moral failure as desiring the wrong kind of food.

In her book *Seeking the Straight and Narrow*, Lynne Gerber focuses on the overlap between these two types of embodied desire, explaining how evangelical weight-loss programs and ex-gay ministries understand bodies as easily disordered by desires for food and sex. These types of groups affirm a set of theological claims that situate bodies as untrustworthy guides toward wholeness that require regular course correction. As such, bodies must be disciplined both physically and spiritually in order to remain under the control of human will. Purity culture, Christian weight-loss programs, and ex-gay ministries all see the human body as suspect, a guide easily corrupted by desires and appetites. Each of these campaigns creates a scenario that presses believers into bodily disciplines that assume animosity between the body, the soul, and the intellect or will.[12] Each demonstrates how evangelicals rely upon a theology of disembodiment that reflects Christianity's historical discomfort with the body as a location of knowledge about the divine. Centuries after classical philosophers and early church fathers battled to control sexuality in the early church, evangelical Christians remain compelled by the belief that bodies have no inherent value beyond their ability to perform holiness. If bodies fail in their expression of religious piety, they become impediments to the same.

In her book *See Me Naked: Stories of Sexual Exile in American Christianity*, Amy Frykholm profiles a young woman she calls Ashley. A very serious evangelical Christian starting in her teen years, Ashley invests in purity culture to demonstrate how the denial of bodily appetites connects food and sex for young women seeking holiness. Before she developed anorexia nervosa in college, Ashley was a high school student bent on perfecting the modesty standards set by organizations like True Love Waits and Joshua Harris's purity manual, *I Kissed Dating Goodbye*. She explained to her mother that she needed to get rid of all the tank tops in her wardrobe because "from now on I am going to dress modestly. I don't want guys looking at me and thinking impure thoughts." Purity culture compelled Ashley to navigate adolescent sexuality by creating the circumstances that would allow her to ignore sexual desire altogether. She learned to discipline herself around appetites, believing that concealing her body with over-sized clothes, denying the need for physical touch, and training herself to ignore her body's communication system would help her achieve spiritual perfection.[13]

When she began replicating this strategy in order to control her food intake, Ashley was well-practiced at avoiding the prompts of her body. Purity culture had given her a road map for achieving disembodiment as it taught her to dismiss and fear natural and necessary appetites. Once in recovery, she had to relearn how to communicate with her body. She had lost the ability to acknowledge physical hunger—to be able to say "I am hungry." She resisted her diagnosis, as she couldn't understand how she could be sick when she had been obediently denying her body—as instructed by her religious community—for so long.

Ashley's, Cynda's, and Anna's eating disorders, Caroline's junior high school modesty checks, Shelly's belief that being sexually pure was her most important asset as a young woman, Nicole learning to be obedient to God's commands—all indicate a set of teachings that encourage women to treat their bodies and bodily desires with fear and disdain. Obedience becomes an act of discipline that demonstrates the will's dominance over the body. Yet, evangelical gender norms allow young men their physical desires, a contradiction that Gilder and Dobson reconcile with their assertion that human civilization requires a strict complementary relationship between the sexes. Their model justifies the monitoring of young women's bodies and appetites, teaching them to self-monitor as an act of religious piety. All of this is in service to a patriarchal system of authority within White evangelicalism in which the structure of the family is expected to mirror the authority of God, with fatherhood situated as nearest to the divine source. All my interviewees were acutely aware of having been raised in patriarchal religion and as adults, many with their own families, had come to realize that they did not want to replicate it.

In the United States, patriarchal religion is a form of authoritarianism that is often associated with Islam and other religions that White evangelicals define themselves against and as superior to. But to do so they have to overlook significant evidence of harmful and abusive dynamics within their own communities, many of which are normalized so as to appear consistent with their own religious teachings. My interviews offer important insights into the work that former evangelicals who experienced patriarchal authority within their churches and families must do in order to no longer feel held accountable by a religious system they no longer believe or participate in. Part of the challenge for people moving away from patriarchal evangelicalism is leaving a community that claims to be altruistically devoted to family life as a center for personal thriving. As one of my research participants remarked, evangelicals who promote purity culture do not recognize their beliefs and practices as harmful. Fay described purity culture as one in which "women are controllable and controlled," and "those inside of purity culture would never admit to being controlling and manipulative and misogynist and sexist. They don't see that. They see themselves as righteous and yet [they are] supremely oppressive."[14]

Kelli's therapist helped her understand the concept of the double bind in order to better understand the impact of her father's authoritarian parenting style (common among families who embrace Christian patriarchy as the biblical model):

> He would give you this list of rules that were impossible, and the goalposts always moved. So, for example, you want me to get from where I am in Pasadena to downtown Los Angeles. And you want me to do it in thirty minutes, but I can't use a car. I can't ride a horse. I can't run. I can't ride a bike. So you're putting all of these kinds of rules around it, making it impossible for me to get to the goal you have set for me. But when I don't meet that goal, and everyone around me is going, well, she never had a chance . . . you just didn't try hard enough. And that's very much how it felt, like there're all these impossible goals and no real tools to get where I'm supposed to be.[15]

Though Kelli wasn't talking only about sexual purity, her metaphor is one of the most apt I encountered in my interviews. The expectations of purity culture are impossible standards meant to remind one of their dependency on God and other authority figures. And yet, young White evangelical women in particular cling to these expectations in hopes of being seen as good and therefore worthy of romantic love. When Harris published *I Kissed Dating Goodbye*, it popularized the practice of courtship. One of the features of courtship culture is saving your first kiss until the wedding day, a practice that became the high watermark of Christian piety among purity advocates. This act of fidelity to God's plan was accompanied by a promise that God will bless the faithful with a marriage of relational and sexual bliss. However, purity culture teachings provide little help for young people navigating real relationships and desires. The romantic idealism, paired with Christian piety, overshadows the hard work of human relating and making sense of one's sexuality, both experiences that often include missteps and a process of learning from mistakes. Purity, Kelli and others learned, was a path to perfection but one that only reminded those walking it of just how imperfect they were.

Leah discussed how the patriarchal Christianity she was raised in set her and other women up for failure: "It basically made women second-class citizens by setting up a whole generation of women for failure, essentially, because anything we did with any boyfriend anywhere at any time basically would lead to shame and guilt. And you just carry that with you."[16] Like Kelli, Leah still struggled as an adult and a mother with carrying the burden of purity culture, even though she fully rejected those beliefs and practices in her own family. She had been taught to fear sex and to see men's sexuality as predatory and dangerous. Many of the women I interviewed described long-term efforts to restore a healthy relationship to their own bodies and sexuality. As a system of control, patriarchal Christianity thrives on monitoring behaviors and relationships and teaches young people that self-monitoring is a form of obedience to God. For Kelli, this meant that "the way you think needs to be monitored, the way you feel needs to be monitored. . . . You either are pure or you're not pure." Purity culture works on a moral binary system, offering clear distinctions for what is acceptable and what is unacceptable. This makes it easy for patriarchal religious communities to maintain boundaries between in-groups and out-groups. In order to be in the group and receive the benefits of the close-knit relationships on offer you must conform to its expectations.

It's often only after leaving their former evangelical contexts that people recognize the degree to which purity teachings have informed their understandings of sex and gender. The patriarchal structure of evangelical family life depends on purity teachings to socialize young people into a narrow set of ideas about sex, dating, and marriage so that they will replicate the same family system as the adults in their communities. Lisa explained it this way, "Evangelicals base a fair amount of their identity and cultural norms on sex, like sex is the basis for marriage, period. Which I didn't really comprehend. I don't think you can comprehend it when you're in it until you've talked to people who have more healthy concepts of sex, but it's like, it's the basis of all interactions between genders, between men and women."[17] Once outside of evangelicalism Lisa was able to understand that she was socialized into a world of mandatory heterosexuality—in which partnering with someone of the opposite sex to have children with was a communal obligation.

The glaring inconsistencies of patriarchal evangelical family life teachings were not lost on my interviewees. They have had to teach themselves how to detect actual dangers in the form of sexual and gender-based violence while also unlearning long-standing fears of sexuality. Jessica explained this well when she described how she learned to "demonize" premarital sex as if it would cast her into an oblivion of relational and sexual chaos. But even as Jessica was learning to fear sex, she was being fed a steady diet of romantic mythologies around marriage. Introducing an apt example of misogyny, she described how she was both taught to fear sex and to also pine for the romantic promises of finding "this perfect man that God has ordained for you."[18]

Lisa, who has conducted her own research on purity culture, made the most direct connection between patriarchal Christianity and purity culture: "Evangelical purity culture as a system . . . is focused on both the structural political power level but equally as much on the intimate, personal familial, relational level. And that control ties both of those levels in ways that I think make it a wildly unique system in the world." Lisa was not the only After Purity Project participant to describe purity culture as both a symptom and a part of the infrastructure of patriarchal evangelicalism. As a system of gender-based oppression it functions in coordination with other forms of inequality that are normalized in White evangelical family life. Angela explained it this way, "[Purity culture] is also hearing sermons and radio shows and TV and movies constantly talk about an image of a family relationship, in a way that feels like brainwashing. The White nuclear family, it becomes the only way to exist in the world that reinforces your own internalized racism and misogyny and homophobia, or it can start to make you question whether you should exist at all since you are outside of that."[19]

For my interviewees, evangelical purity culture used romantic mythologies to secure their innocence as Christian teenagers who learned to fear and dismiss their bodies as sources of information, wisdom, and pleasure. Purity teachings made disembodiment a sacrament, a way to demonstrate one's fitness for salvation. Each one of my interviewees understood the intimacy of its impact well into adulthood, including marriage, divorce, and whatever came next. And many understood that relational hardship was not the worst of the purity-culture aftermath. Evangelical purity culture was presented as having a commitment to caring for young people by cultivating spiritual habits divorced from bodily desire. But in practice it contributed to a larger culture in which young men and especially young women learned to distrust their bodies and their own intuitions. Under the guise of innocence preservation and divine authority, purity teachings became a chapter in an authoritarian playbook, one dedicated to controlling women and children and exonerating the men who did them harm.

CHAPTER TWO

POWER AND ABUSE

O N JANUARY 9, 2022, Pastor Rusty Chatfield had a difficult church service ahead of him. His eldest son, Lee Chatfield, former Michigan state congressman, had been accused of sexual assault by his sister-in-law, a story that went public shortly after she filed the complaint against him. Rebecca Chatfield's relationship with the family began when she was a young teenager and a student at Northern Michigan Christian Academy, founded by Pastor Chatfield. She was drawn to the tight knit, family-based, Christian community in the state's Upper Peninsula because of stresses within her own family. She described this to the media outlet *Bridge Michigan* after she filed her complaint. Lee Chatfield has used her vulnerability to manipulate and prey on her starting when Rebecca was fifteen.[1]

Pastor Chatfield, the family patriarch who founded the academy and the Northern Michigan Bible Baptist Church, created an environment where he and other men spoke the word of a stern and exacting God in order to extract obedience from students and congregants. At one point, Rebecca's mother pulled her from the school when she realized the community enforced strict compliance with authoritarian gender roles, including obedience to the pastor, teachers, and other men in authority, including a young Lee Chatfield.

Though the presence of purity teachings within an evangelical community does not necessarily equate with the presence of abuse, the gender roles prescribed for biblical obedience indicate a culture in which abuse can emerge and persist. The most recent studies on evangelical purity culture examine its relationship to rape culture and how acceptance of purity teachings is closely linked to myths about rape. Evangelical purity culture promotes the sexual and emotional passivity of young women and accepts, even promotes, the belief that young men have voracious sexual appetites that women and girls are expected to control. This means that groups that endorse purity culture are more likely to disbelieve claims of marital rape and acquaintance rape. Purity culture, as Rebecca Chatfield learned, is designed to endorse male-headship and provide cover for men and boys, who are allowed to indulge their sexual desires.[2]

For young women like Rebecca, who sought security and belonging within evangelicalism, the tension between the obligation to remain sexually pure and the experience of normal adolescent sexual desire is disorientating. For women like Rebecca, that tension, coupled with the expectation to obey men in authority, provides few options for securing their future beyond appealing to the men in their orbit.

While Rebecca sought security and belonging while also navigating the advances of a sexual predator, a young Lee Chatfield was being primed for a leadership role. In the small community presided over by this father, Chatfield's authority, competence, and integrity went unquestioned and his indiscretions ignored. Chatfield taught and coached at Northern Michigan Christian Academy, where Rebecca was a student, and he held a position of authority where they regularly interacted. While there are many models of Christian schooling, the family-based model of Rusty Chatfield's Christian academy was designed to consolidate the power of the Chatfield family. Lee's wife, Stephanie, teaches K–5, and Rusty Chatfield serves as both school superintendent and a history teacher in the upper grades.

The week in January 2022 when the allegations against Lee went public, Pastor Chatfield preached a sermon without mentioning his son or the accusations against him, speaking obliquely about "certain circumstances."[3] His sermon exhibited the common symptoms of evangelical communities reeling from sexual misconduct allegations against their leaders:

1. Cast blame elsewhere (the enemy, the accuser, the media)
2. Emphasize sin as a universal human trait
3. Affirm biblical beliefs as superseding other forms of law

Chatfield chided his church members not to believe everything they read in the paper or on the internet, and he reminded them of what he referred to as their " unique calling" as Christians to build a church and school and to stand for the truth. However, Chatfield stumbled in his ability to identify what the truth was in his son's story.

Truth will come forward. Eventually truth will come forward. What they are saying here, there is a measure of truth. I like to say there was one-third truth. It is reported—that's the anonymous source thing [...] with no one verifying the truth. But that's what sells newspapers.

There is a measure of truth here. Even for Christians—sometimes we sin. We know we all have sinned and come short of the glory of God. We are all sinners. Sin happens. And all of you know that is the way it is. You've seen it here. You've seen it other places.

The church of Jesus Christ is full of sinners. You got to know that. Parts of things are true. And parts are not true. And the enemy is always lying, distorting. Some truth. And some not truth. So some of it is true.[4]

Northern Michigan Bible Baptist Church is not a mega-church headed by a celebrity pastor. The church and school, with a barely usable website, are both indicative of the characteristic modesty of northern Michigan and its residents. Regardless, this place was the launching pad for Lee Chatfield, whose status as a pastor's son in a small evangelical community allowed him leadership opportunities that would eventually land him in the Michigan state legislature.

What is clear is that the elder Chatfield was unwilling to acknowledge the possibility that his son's behaviors caused harm. Furthermore, he described the allegations as an attack by "the enemy" to distract the church from its work, again using vague language to describe his church's mission. The lack of a clear statement of purpose or service mission by a church often indicates that a religious community is primarily concerned about bringing people under a canopy of surveillance and obedience, the idea being that "this is what God has commissioned us to do." Reverend Chatfield's impulse to close ranks and warn his followers that the enemy is near is not an act of service to his flock but a fearful proclamation that everything he has built may soon be revealed as a breeding ground for the sexual predator who is his son.

By 1994 True Love Waits had gained national attention and hundreds of thousands of faithfully committed followers.[5] Within two years, it would boast numbers in the millions. The rollout was intentionally grandiose, calling Christ-following teenagers to live a pure and holy life free of guilt, shame, and romantic disappointment. Striving for sexual purity became a moral mandate, mapped onto the adolescent believer's path to salvation, a path fraught with the dangers of secular temptation, physical pleasure, and immediate gratification.

TLW framed itself as an oasis and a refuge for adolescents from the threats of secular life. It characterized church life as a community with the highest of moral expectations but equally secure support systems to protect and accompany young people on their passage to adulthood, i.e., heterosexual, Christian marriage. TLW and evangelical purity culture as a whole provided a clear demarcation: The secular world is fraught with sexual danger and heartbreak. Their world was blessed with sexual safety and the promise of true love.

The emergence of evangelical purity culture (and its meteoric rise to national prominence) was a means for evangelicals to seek and maintain political power. A moral panic fueled by HIV/AIDS and teen pregnancy made groups like TLW appear salvific in their approach to human sexuality. The promise of sexual safety appealed to adults, while that of emotional and sexual fulfillment appealed to the young.

Purity campaigns increased the political influence of evangelicalism and its male leadership. They originated in the same decade that fundamentalist leaders reinstated authoritarianism and gender hierarchies at all Southern Baptist churches and seminaries, systematically removing women from leadership positions over the next several decades.[6] When understood in conjunction with the fundamentalist takeover in the denomination, True Love Waits was developed to socialize young men and women into a culture of female submission and male authority. Lacking any commitment to female empowerment and gender equality, purity campaigns became the staging ground for sexual abuse and institutional neglect toward women and girls.

In 2019, the *Houston Chronicle* published a series of articles detailing two decades of clergy sex abuse within the SBC, along with the denomination's proclaimed inability to address the problem. In response to survivor advocates, who demanded that the denomination keep track of employees charged with sexual misconduct, the SBC claimed it had a limited ability to do so because of the denomination's congregationalist structure in which local churches remain autonomous. While organizational structures, policies, and practices are complex, it should be mentioned that despite the decentralization of their ecclesiastical structure, the SBC had little problem growing TLW into an international movement with significant political and social influence at the very same time the denomination was failing to protect its young people from sexual predators.

Christa Brown, a lawyer and a survivor of childhood sexual abuse perpetrated by her youth minister, has been at the forefront of calling the SBC to account for almost two decades. As a teenager, Brown was groomed by Pastor Tommy Gilmore, who gave her extra attention, pushed her physical boundaries, and spent time alone with her until declaring that he was obsessed with her.[7] He fawned over her, telling her how much he and God loved her. She struggled with deeply conflicting feelings. He declared that they were married in the eyes of God and could now prepare themselves to be married on Earth. Never mind that Pastor Gilmore was already married with children. When she expressed concern about remaining a virgin, he gave her an uninformed opinion about human sexuality. "It's only sex if it can make you pregnant," and he went on to explain that as long as her hymen remained intact, she was still a virgin. Brown felt special and chosen, so when Pastor Tommy told her they needed to keep their relationship secret, she did so. But when he became angry with her for cutting her hair, she felt compelled to confide in a friend about his displeasure in her choice. Her friend's response was not disgust or confusion but awe. When Brown and her friend were in the eighth grade, an older girl in their youth group married a former youth minister of theirs. Without any consideration for the origins of that relationship or age of consent laws, Brown and her friend found the idea of a relationship with a minister deeply romantic. "It must be God's will," Christa's friend assured her about her relationship with Pastor Tommy.

Soon, though, Pastor Tommy began accusing Brown of having seduced him and of being a temptress. Brown believed him and convinced herself she was deserving of damnation. Burdened with shame, she confessed to her piano instructor, the church's music minister, that she was having what she called an affair with Pastor Tommy. Though her instructor never spoke to her about it again, Pastor Tommy was quickly removed from the church with no explanation for his departure. Before he left, Pastor Tommy made Brown apologize to his wife, explaining that the entire extramarital affair had been her fault.

It wasn't until Brown had her own sixteen-year-old daughter that she gained clarity about her relationship with Pastor Tommy. She was stunned to realize that by labeling her experiences with him an affair, she had ignored the age and power discrepancies of their relationship. After years of experiencing psychological distress, Brown was finally able to describe that relationship accurately: she was groomed and raped by an adult leader in her church. It is not uncommon for sexual assault survivors to take many decades to piece together an accurate account of what happened to them.

Christa Brown published her account in 2009, not because she needed to expose her abuser (she refrained from using his name at the time) but because she felt compelled to expose the entire church institution that protected Pastor Tommy and its own reputation.[8] Five years earlier she had reported the abuse to her former church. In their written response, crafted by the church's attorney, they denied her claims. "Rarely is a single individual in possession of all the facts necessary to make an informed judgement.... You do not assert that there were reports of any incidents of alleged inappropriate conduct involving Mr. Gilmore. [...] There are many reasons why your client has suffered emotionally, which are not attributable to the actions of Mr. Gilmore or the church."[9] The church's response only emboldened Christa to dig further into Gilmore's whereabouts, and she discovered, decades after she reported the abuse, that her abuser was still working as a youth minister in the SBC. She also discovered that the SBC in Texas had been keeping tabs on clergy who were convicted or confessed to sexual abuse, yet remained unwilling to make that information available, even to church hiring committees. With these revelations and her own legal expertise, Brown demanded accountability in a 2009 op-ed in the *Dallas Morning News* that called for the SBC to make its clergy-abuse database available.[10] When her request was denied, she started her own public list using data from multiple survivors who contacted her in response to the op-ed. This is how Christa Brown became a survivor advocate and a righteous thorn in the side of the Southern Baptist Convention.

In recent years, Brown's work has been reinforced by other survivors going public with their stories. You can find many of them on social media using the platforms to disclose their abuse and the various Christian institutions that perpetrated all manner of cover-ups, denials, and attacks. However, it was the release of the *Houston Chronicle* series "Abuse of Faith" that revealed the widespread nature of the issue. The *Chronicle* also created its own database of clergy abusers, which has been publicly available since 2017.[11] However, the list alone does not tell the stories of the cover-ups, spiritual manipulation, and denialism among SBC leadership that many survivors experienced, which is why journalists produced numerous articles featuring their stories. But even the *Chronicle*'s extensive reporting could not exhaust the incidents of sexual and religious exploitation within the largest evangelical denomination in the US.

The case of Paige Patterson was one rare indication that the SBC is willing to hold its own accountable. The former president of the denomination and one of the men who enforced the fundamentalist takeover in the 1980s, Patterson served twice as president of two denominational seminaries and had a reputation for misogyny. He celebrated abused women staying in their marriages in order to bring their husbands to Christ, and he sexualized a young woman as part of a sermon illustration. In 2018, Patterson lost his position as president of Southwestern Baptist Theological Seminary (SBTS) for this behavior, but the firing initially included a generous compensation package, including the title president emeritus.[12] Shortly after, the board of trustees at SBTS received a complaint from Megan Lively, a former student at Southeastern Baptist Theological Seminary. Megan was enrolled in the SBTS's Women's Studies program, designed by Patterson's wife to educate young women about their "biblical roles" as mothers and wives, when she was sexually assaulted by another student she was dating.[13]

Lively described to the board what happened after she reported her assault to the student office on campus, saying that Patterson had contacted her immediately after she reported the assault. She said he questioned her, asking for precise details of the incident and suggesting that Lively was responsible for what had happened. He counseled her to not contact the police and to forgive her rapist. Upon learning this, the board of trustees revoked Patterson's retirement package, including the emeritus title.[14]

In 2021, SBC leadership allowed an independent investigation by Guideposts Solution, which released its findings a year later.[15] The report confirmed what many already knew: not only was there an epidemic of sexual and gender-based violence within the denomination, but leaders had spent years denying and accusing survivors of lying, causing division, and even being demonic. The report allowed numerous survivors the opportunity to share their stories, including a pastor's wife who was raped by her husband's colleague, a prominent clergy member. The report also noted that the SBC had been keeping a secret list of accused and convicted perpetrators, which it had claimed they were unable to do when survivors began requesting it well over a decade prior.

Shortly after the report's release, the church body voted overwhelmingly to create Ministry Check, a centralized database to track abusers, and a permanent committee to handle sex-abuse accusations going forward. Despite this mandate from their membership, the SBC Executive Committee remain unwilling and unable to adopt accountability practices, in particular an open database alerting churches to religious leaders with criminal sexual histories. In 2024, the SBC's sexual abuse task force responsible for creating and enforcing accountability practices, ended its efforts claiming lack of funding and insurance complications.[16] At its most recent meeting, in January 2025, the executive committee announced that the Ministry Check database it had proposed was no long a priority.[17]

With the emergence of the MeToo movement it became clear that the SBC and many other evangelical churches were far behind the learning curve when it came to sexual and gender-based violence. Fortunately, in 2017, the world came to know the name Tarana Burke, an activist and advocate who at that point had worked alongside survivors of sexual assault for over a decade. Though her work entered the public eye by White celebrity women seeking to address the problem of assault in the entertainment industry, Burke's MeToo movement changed everything about the way we think, speak, and process experiences of sexual assault. And while our institutions and communities continue to struggle with acknowledging the deep-seated and widespread nature of the problem and its roots in evangelical purity culture, others of us are learning a new language grounded in bodily autonomy and consent.

Like many survivors, Emily Joy Allison was following the MeToo movement with great interest. Her body understood what it felt like to be a survivor, even if her mind had struggled to comprehend that what she experienced as an adolescent was, in fact, abuse. Allison was targeted by an adult youth minister who fed her compliments and showered her with attention until he started a relationship with her, which she was instructed to keep secret. She was fifteen, and he was in his early thirties. However, because she never had a physical relationship with him, Allison struggled to name the nature of the trauma she felt so clearly in her body: grooming. She describes this experience in her book, *#ChurchToo: How Purity Culture Upholds Abuse and How to Find Healing*:

> He started singling me out early—paying me compliments, giving me more responsibilities than the other students, and even going so far as to pay me for doing nonchurch work for him, such as proofreading copy for websites he'd been contracted to build. Conversations slowly drifted from how to set up layers in InDesign to who I was dating, and I became accustomed, as many of the students did, to discussing the intimate details of my romantic life, what little there was, with him. He styled himself as a mentor and gave advice in a way that implied you'd be awfully foolish to do otherwise. In what I now recognize to be classic predatory grooming behavior, he even convinced me to break up with the person I was dating at fifteen.[18]

One night, emboldened by good friends and glass of rosé, Allison decided it was time to out her abuser on social media. She crafted a clear, direct post that offered readers an expanded understanding of sexual abuse and included the hashtag #ChurchToo. When she woke up the next morning, she found that her post had gone viral, with hundreds of others retweeting #ChurchToo and sharing their experiences of grooming, abuse, and assault within their religious communities.

Before 2017, clergy sexual assault was a set of scandals associated mostly with the Roman Catholic Church and waxy-haired television preachers. That all changed because of #ChurchToo and the *Houston Chronicle* "Abuse of Faith" series. For many who followed the SBC, and especially its history of silencing and threatening survivors, this was not bombshell material, but it was a new opening for survivors to bring their cases to public view and increase pressure on the denomination to enact change.

The *Houston Chronicle* database uncovered sexual abuser Chad Foster, a youth minister at Houston's Second Baptist Church who taught abstinence and encouraged teenagers to sign the True Love Waits Commitment Card, while at the same time he was soliciting teenage girls at the church's camp with text messages and "physical contact," according to the *Chronicle*.[19] He was fired from his position in 2010 based on complaints from his coworkers and congregants. But church leadership gave no reasons for his firing to the congregation or the youth group, nor did they pass on the information to the next church where Foster was hired as a youth pastor. Court records show Foster attempted inappropriate relationships with teenage girls in that church as well.

According to the *Chronicle*, more than a hundred SBC youth ministers in numerous states have been charged with sex crimes, are imprisoned, and/or are on the federal sex-offenders registry. True Love Waits was a campaign designed for youth ministry. It became a full-fledged gospel message, one that all but replaced the traditional gospel message focused on obedience to God. Obey God's commands to be sexually pure and all your romantic ideals will be fulfilled. The message was straightforward and theologically simple. It was created in a vacuum where ignorance and denial of sexual abuse abounded.

The one place where TLW attempted to address the issue of sexual assault offers insight into how purity teachings promote a culture of abuse. A thirty-page pamphlet authored by Richard Ross and Tony Rankin, entitled *When True Love Doesn't Wait*, is the only source published by the organization that addresses the topic.[20] Its contents reveal a great deal about how these teachings echo the views that characterize rape culture. The pamphlet first argues that sex is always a danger that needs to be controlled, thereby placing the burden of responsibility on young people learning to navigate their own sexual desire. "You probably know that sex before marriage breaks God's law and is a serious sin. You may honestly wonder what the future holds for someone who could do such a thing." Sex before marriage, Ross and Rankin claim, is a catastrophic event on par with violent acts. "Once a person has been through a tornado, fire, shooting or sexual experience, a memory is created." Adolescents who have positive sexual experiences are encouraged to reframe them as harmful. Sex goes from being a curiosity to a natural disaster. If sex before marriage is always a disaster, how do young people learn to recognize when they are experiencing real harm?

The authors also ascribe destructive behaviors such as drug and alcohol use to adolescent sexual guilt. "Guilty teenagers give up completely, exercise some method of escape: drugs, sex, alcohol, or withdrawal from life." Ross and Rankin fail to see that the "dangerous behaviors" they describe can also be efforts to cope with various forms of trauma. Instead, they participate in victim blaming, saying these habits are the result of guilt accrued from disobeying God's command not to have sex outside of marriage.

The authoritarian logic of True Love Waits adheres to the patterns of institutional abuse studied by scholars and survivor advocates. According to Stephanie Krehbiel and Hilary Jerome Scarsella of Into

Account, an advocacy organization for survivors of sexual assault in religious communities, Christian theological teachings can and do promote cultures of abuse. It requires understanding that sexual abuse is both deeply personal and embedded in institutional norms. Christian theologies that valorize suffering, service, and obedience create a culture in which the value and worth of individuals is based on their ability to comply with these signifiers of Christian piety. These same theologies become a sinister force in the life of abuse survivors who struggle to regain safety and self-worth.

When True Love Doesn't Wait assures its readers that being forced to have sex does not mean the loss of one's virginity. Valorizing virginity, Ross and Rankin offer it as a tool for supposedly helping survivors recover from their assault. Then they go on to say this, "Reporting this immediately will increase your believability. Unfortunately, some persons use this excuse once they've been caught, find out someone is pregnant, or discover an STD. Your reason for reporting is not to get the other person in trouble."

This paragraph offers insight into how TLW and the SBC think about survivorship. It serves as check list for "good survivors" who want to be believed and taken seriously. The assumption being, if you do not follow these directives your experiences can be dismissed, and we will conclude you are committing libel against your brother in Christ, thus justifying the harassment of survivors. To put this more plainly, Ross and Rankin are promoting rape culture, which believes that survivors use rape accusations as a cover for their own guilt over sexual activity. The solution Ross and Rankin offer is not to hold perpetrators accountable but for victims to follow their instructions so that the powers that be can determine if a survivor's allegations are true or a cover for their own sinful behavior.

Ross, Rankin, and every youth minister who endorses sexual purity will claim they have always done so out of love for young people and their spiritual thriving. They claim that the goal of sexual purity is to protect young people from harmful relationships and self-hatred. But reading Ross and Rankin's words and seeing how little they understand about sexual survivorship, I'm left wondering: what did they know? Did they know of the proliferation of sexual abusers in the church? Did they know they needed a way to address it without drawing attention to the failures of the institution? What if the purpose of TLW was to make the vulnerable population feel responsible for their own sexual safety hopes they could better defend themselves from sexual predators? I don't have the answer to these questions, and I suspect many in the SBC would throw me under the same bus they use to flatten survivors. But advocating for survivors requires digging into the depths of the unthinkable, something the SBC leadership has been unwilling to do, and they still haven't adequately explained why.

Within most White evangelical communities, a reckoning with sexual violence is barely underway. As a racialized, Christian faith tradition, White evangelicalism bends believers toward obedience and silence in service to vague notions of orthodoxy or biblical truth. Within such religious systems, sexual violence is a disruption, but greater protest emerges when a survivor demands to be believed and seeks justice for the wrong committed against her. It is a feature of survivorship within White evangelicalism that seeking comfort and consolation from one's religious community causes more, not less, suffering, as survivors frequently experience re-traumatization in the form of disbelief, blame, and shame.

Ann is one such case.[21] During our interview I encountered a solid, energetic, red-headed mom whose battle for justice was only betrayed by the occasional wry tone in her voice. Ann was a victim of childhood sexual assault and incest who, at the age of thirteen, sought understanding and support from her youth minister, who subsequently assaulted her. In the aftermath, her thirty-year-old abuser claimed that she had initiated contact, that she was demon-possessed, and that she should be shunned. Prior to her assault, Ann loved her church youth group, one of the few places where she felt safe and that she belonged. That changed quickly as it seemed everyone, including her peers and her own mother, believed she was to blame for the "sexual encounter." They pointed to her behavior, especially her need for attention from church leaders, and even her red hair as indicative of a seductive personality.

Ann understands now that the behavior that the adults in her life labeled "seductive" was a trauma response. Ann learned to gain the attention of boys in order to secure protection for herself, a psychosocial need provoked by her earliest experiences of abuse. But to others, it appeared as if she was making herself sexually available to them, generating a degree of criticism reserved for novels about uptight Puritan communities. By misidentifying Ann as the perpetrator, her community failed to recognize survivor behavior that requires compassionate care. Instead, the community used the tenets of purity culture to shame and ostracize her. Even worse, they failed to recognize that their trusted youth minister was abusing both his authority and a young teenager.

This is the work of evangelical purity culture: it allows communities to misidentify the locus of sexual misconduct, allowing their values and beliefs to remain intact. Ann's congregation used boundary marking (labeling, shunning) in order to maintain the virtue of the entire community. The church's view was that a young, female adolescent unable to control her urges is a problem solved by a renewed commitment to purity culture. A religious professional who exploits a vulnerable young person is an entirely different matter, one that requires investigating deep-seated problems that raise questions about communal identity and theological principles that can easily unmoor a church or family.

Even more incredible to me is that of all the people I interviewed, Ann is among those who have remained Christian, who values her current church community, and who is raising her children according to the teachings of Jesus. With this support system in place, she was able to bring criminal charges against her former youth pastor.

There are only seven states in the US where felony sexual assault has no statute of limitations. In Canada, where Ann lives and attends church, there is no such statute, which allowed Ann to bring charges twenty years after her rape.

Reporting and prosecuting sexual assault and abuse often mean that survivors have to brace themselves for accusation, dismissal, and new layers of trauma on top of the old. For many survivors, trauma disrupts memory, so even being able to craft a narrative in which they can tell the truth about their experiences (especially to themselves) is in itself a feat. So what Ann was able to do was in all ways remarkable. Even more remarkable, in October 2023, her abuser's appeal for a retrial was denied by the court system. As she wrote on social media: "[His] appeal has been denied. 3 years after I went to the police, I am exiting the Canadian court system with a win under my belt, firm and final."

Research that helps us understand the dynamics of sexual assault within religious communities draws on two overlapping forms of trauma: religious and sexual. While sexual trauma has been widely studied and well-integrated into mental health care, religious trauma remains somewhat unexplored territory. Laura Anderson, a psychotherapist with expertise in religious trauma, has worked in this field for many years, growing a practice that includes the Center for Trauma Resolution and Recovery, which offers services specifically for people seeking to recover from evangelical purity culture. When I talked with Anderson in the spring of 2021, she explained that purity teachings impact our brains and bodies in the same way other forms of abuse evoke embodied responses. However, unlike the experiences of physical or sexual assault, victims cannot point to a particular moment during their time in purity culture when the impact began, beyond enduring the grooming, abuse, and assault. Processing trauma, Anderson said, requires building a narrative around the experience, especially since trauma survivors often struggle with memory and since purity culture is often experienced not as a specific event but as years of socialization into a series of beliefs and practices that control people's agency. Processing this kind of trauma is much more difficult as there is no clear starting point. Anderson explained further that purity culture is not simply about sex but rather is a wide-ranging ethic that divides behaviors, attitudes, and practices into good and bad. It is a surveillance system that evaluates everything: choice of clothing, media intake, friend groups. The result of living under purity surveillance is what Anderson and others in her field call *complex developmental trauma*, which undermines personal agency, including the ability to extract oneself from a rigid moral system.

Not surprisingly, the effort to recover and move away from the exacting pressures of purity culture is not an easy one. As noted above, even after an individual has retracted their adherence to purity teachings, the bodily prompts remain intact. When anxiety and guilt have been attached to sexual desire for so long, the work to separate the two is significant. It's no surprise to me that mental health professionals such as Anderson are overwhelmed with clients seeking her assistance in their efforts to recover bodily autonomy and sexual pleasure.

Anderson's work describes how difficult it can be to distinguish between sexual and religious trauma, especially in the context of purity culture. In clinical psychology and related fields, religion is overwhelming identified as having a positive impact on individual well-being because it provides meaning-making, emotional stability, and built-in community support. However, for a growing number of people with adverse experiences in their religious communities, the need for resources and trained experts addressing religious trauma is growing exponentially, especially among the generation of people raised within purity culture.

Though all of my research participants discussed adverse experiences within purity culture, most did not describe experiences of sexual abuse. I don't know if is appropriate to ascribe *survivorship* to all people who have grown up and out of purity culture, a term that is used to designate people who have survived high-control religious communities and sexual abuse in any context. My research participants demonstrated the many ways they resisted purity culture teachings, some having done so beginning in their adolescence. For others, it took being away from their religious community of origin, becoming sexually active, getting married, becoming a parent, and/or mental health counseling to be able to name the harm they continue to experience and seek to understand. Complex developmental trauma, as Laura Anderson describes above, demands significant emotional labor. By the time many sat down to speak with me, they had already been telling their stories, or at least crafting the narrative for themselves. The ability to piece together a narrative of harm that accurately describes one's experiences with purity culture and abuse indicates positive change toward trauma healing and recovery. In this process, individuals have to rewire their thinking around culpability and shame and replace it with the understanding that purity culture was never about being a good Christian but about being manipulated into accepting disembodiment as a spiritual practice. Even if they reported no sexual or religious abuse, all my respondents pointed to experiences within family, church, dating, and friendships that left them devastated, confused, and betrayed.

Within a decade of True Love Waits saturating youth culture, both within and outside the church, there was a swift reprisal against its teachings. Early critics, like writers Sarah Bessey and Rachel Held Evans, seemed to indicate a new wave of evangelical feminism challenging purity culture and the "idolization of virginity" that it promoted.[22] Opposition would increase exponentially because of Elizabeth Smart, whose story of abduction and rape included a description of how purity teachings from her church impaired her ability to seek rescue from her situation.

In 2002, fourteen-year-old Elizabeth Smart was abducted at knifepoint from her home in Salt Lake City, held captive, and raped multiple times over nine months. As a young Mormon, Smart had learned that sex outside of marriage was incompatible with her physical, emotional, and spiritual integrity. Sex outside of marriage made her feel dirty and unwanted and best suited for the garbage. As an adult, she works as an advocate for survivors of sex-trafficking and in this capacity reflected on how the principles of sexual purity inhibited her ability to flee her captors. Smart explained that once her captors had sexually assaulted her, she believed that her body and her life no longer held value.

> I thought, "Oh my gosh, I'm that chewed-up piece of gum. Nobody rechews a piece of gum; you throw it away." And that's how easy it is to feel like you no longer have worth, you no longer have value. Why would it even be worth screaming out? Why would it even make a difference if you are rescued? Your life still has no value?[23]

The similarities between evangelical purity teachings and the laws of chastity within the LDS church are strikingly similar. When the *Christian Science Monitor* reported Smart's comments, the evangelical blogosphere went to work, not to decry Smart's criticism of sexual purity but to affirm it. The metaphor of chewed gum resonated with young evangelicals, who themselves had been an audience to similar metaphors, including wooden hearts hacked by chainsaws, tongues ripped from frozen flag poles, and toothpaste squeezed from the tube (you can never put it back in). These metaphors served to reinforce a belief that sexual intercourse outside of marriage is psychologically harmful and that a commitment to sexual purity is in part a formula for achieving psychological well-being.

No, not everyone who grew up in and out of purity culture experienced sexual abuse. But as a series of teachings, purity culture perpetuates a set of rules about human sexuality that normalize abuse: sex outside marriage is dangerous and shameful; men and boys are innately sexually aggressive; women and girls are innately sexually passive, if not entirely uninterested in sex. Each of these rules disempowers girls and young women from understanding themselves as sexual beings and from learning about what sex and sexual desire are. At the same time, these rules offer men and boys a great deal of sexual freedom and normalize their sexual aggression. Coupled with an authoritarian leadership structure and silence around sexual development, purity culture keeps young people from understanding the rights they have to their own bodies. Add a bad actor in the form of a sexual predator or pedophile to this climate and they will find ample opportunity to groom, abuse, and assault.

These rules were reiterated in each and every interview I conducted. While some women had the ability to recognize their problematic nature even as an adolescent, others continued to struggle with significant fear around sex and men, often resulting in an inability to experience sexual pleasure. Purity culture creates an unsafe environment and then requires those most vulnerable to take responsibility for their actions and behaviors in order to protect themselves. Even if the lack of safety didn't result in harm, the sexual danger that pervades purity culture informed young people at the earliest stages of their sexual development, setting them up for an adulthood rife with sexual anxiety and fear.

CHAPTER THREE

EVANGELICAL EXODUS

I GREW UP AN EVANGELICAL CHRISTIAN. Attending a parent-run Christian school in grades K–12, I learned that public schools were inferior and dangerous learning environments. During high school we attended the March for Life, the national anti-abortion protest held every January in Washington, DC, driving nine hours in one day, we marched and stood alongside people carrying posters of dead fetuses. And yes, I understood even before watching those Josh McDowell "Why Wait?" VHS tapes in Sunday school exactly why I should wait to have sex before marriage. As an older teenager I challenged myself to be bold in my faith. At church camp I wanted to share the love of Jesus as we paddled our way through the rapids of the Youghiogheny River. I worried that because I was raised Christian and didn't have a dramatic conversion story or difficulty following the rules of my faith, I wasn't able to offer the story of my life as a testimony.

It was the early 1990s, before True Love Waits and Joshua Harris and purity rings would become ubiquitous in the lives of Christian teenagers. But I understood that not having sex was an essential part of demonstrating my commitment to being a Christian. When an article advocating for comprehensive sex education appeared in my local newspaper, the *Beaver County Times*, I felt the need to be seen and heard. So I crafted a response that was published by my local paper.

A March 22 article reported on the classroom tactics of Cindy Forshee at Ambridge Area High School concerning AIDS, sex, and the whole deal. What really disturbs me about what is being taught in the public schools is that abstinence, the only safe sex, in high school is unrealistic. I attend a Christian high school at which we deal with all of this through programs such as Josh McDowell's "Why Wait?" This series portrays sex as a sacred act which is to be saved for marriage. But, of course, this belief is old-fashioned and unrealistic. However, if this is old-fashioned, why are there high school students who believe in it today? And why, if it is unrealistic, are high school students living it? Maybe if abstinence were presented as a real option, students would consider it more. What's more important, supporting the condom industry or our safety? Think about it!

Setting aside the fact that my memory of this letter did not re-emerge until after I published my first book on purity culture, at the age of forty-one, this relic of my past offers a portrait of a Christian teen on fire for Jesus or at least certain that she was right about everything. The difference was never clear to me.

Despite the incontrovertible evidence of my evangelical bona fides, I never used that word to identify myself. We simply called ourselves Christian with the certainty that we knew who was not. We mocked the Baptists and their hyper-fixation on hem lines and prohibitions against dancing. I squirmed in the presence of Pentecostals and other holiness folks whose churches attracted people who spoke in tongues. And though my mom, sister, and I devoured those Frank Peretti books about spiritual warfare, which portrayed the United Nations as a front for demonic activity, I scoffed at anyone who focused their energies preparing for the end times. My sister and I were kicked out of the

Christian homeschool theatre group because our parents "limited the work of the holy spirit" by asking that their teenage daughters not spend several days a week rehearsing and performing. This decision came to us because of a "spiritual director," who, according to rumors, walked backwards around the barn-converted-theatre in a suspicious cloud of something my Calvinist-soaked mind could not comprehend.

But we never called ourselves evangelicals.

As a US religious historian who has made some contribution to the academic study of evangelicalism in the United States, I have yet to understand this discrepancy, much less this category we call evangelical. Beginning in the 1980s, scholars defined it based on a set of theological beliefs and practices: Jesus-focused, Bible-focused, conversion experience, and sharing the "good news." But by that point White evangelicals in the US were already a political force, aligning themselves with the Republican Party, prompting this teenager from Western Pennsylvania to conclude that in order to be a good Christian, or a Christian at all, one must vote Republican. In retrospect, it almost feels like a ruse to identify evangelicalism as a unique set of theological beliefs since they are, in fact, shared by many other Christian traditions. Even more, a concerted study of the history of evangelicalism demonstrates a diversity of thought around what constitutes "good news."

For me, what is most fascinating about evangelicals and their stern brethren, fundamentalists, is how they define themselves in relationship to what they claim to not be part of: the world. Since the nineteenth century, the butterfly dance between the holy and the profane has allowed evangelicals to maneuver themselves into prominent positions of power and influence. Within the fold, distinctions between the theological, cultural, and political are parsed with the fine-toothed comb of orthodoxy in order to maintain the illusion of a pure faith undiluted by cultural norms and political ideology.

Claims to purity function as imposed boundary markers that are necessary for constructing an insider-outsider dynamic. The work of building and protecting this boundary is, again, not unique to evangelicals, nor even to religion. But in the late twentieth century, evangelical Christians elevated boundary marking and maintenance to a perverse art form that more closely resembled troops assembling for battle than community building among co-religionists.

So perhaps the best way to understand contemporary White evangelicalism is to tell the stories of those who saw through the ruse, stepped outside the evangelical world, and found themselves on the outside of everything they thought they knew about the secular world. In 2016, author and podcaster Blake Chastain named this growing and vocal group of former evangelicals, who had coalesced on social media into a loose-knit community: the ex-vangelicals. Chastain, able to harness the collective grief, confusion, and anger among former evangelicals, also gave a name to the human experience of becoming the other—the thing you were told not to be if you wanted to be happy, successful, and saved.

> Leaving an evangelical community can feel very isolating. Evangelical culture is all-encompassing. If you are "plugged in" to a local evangelical church, chances are that your entire social support network is dependent upon it. Your closest friends and confidantes are consolidated into a group that is, when push comes to shove, highly prejudicial and judgmental. Your acceptance in the group is conditional: believe and behave a certain way, or you will be ostracized, admonished, excommunicated.[1]

The majority of my research participants were adolescent evangelicals in the 1990s–2000s, when megachurches were booming and purity culture was saturating mainstream culture via Disney pop stars. It was an era of "extreme teen" evangelicalism, when teens proudly declared their virginity in public and, in an echo of the Jesus Movement of the 1970s, believed themselves to be making a radical, countercultural choice to follow Jesus. The language of the counterculture was pervasive, with White evangelicals co-opting the language of the civil rights, feminist, and gay rights movements. They cast themselves as outsiders to mainstream cultural and political life in order to co-opt the power that had been hard won by marginalized groups fighting for basic human rights.

Coerced into dismissing their own needs and desires to follow God's will, young evangelicals in these decades were encouraged to live to the extreme, where they would find ultimate meaning. In these decades, evangelicalism became an industry, marketed to young consumers as a complete identity with a built-in community. The sense of belonging, enthusiasm, and all-around good feelings made it especially attractive to anyone whose family life was fraught with danger, who struggled with interpersonal relationships, or just wanted to feel a deep sense of purpose. The affective enticement of evangelicalism is difficult to ignore as it is curated and marketed to elicit emotional responses that, when shared in a large group, create a sense of sacred community that satisfies the need for human intimacy. In the context of worship, the thrall of holy names such as Jesus, God the Father, and the Holy Spirit become points of contact where believers feel safe to give away their own desires and intuition in favor of following and belonging.

For those who've experienced the collective effervescence of charismatic or conversative Christianity, discovering how these worship experiences are used to manipulate believers into perpetuating self-harm and harm against others is a significant blow. Many pass through a stage of deep cynicism, anger, and self-hatred. The Netflix series *Beef* explores the façade of evangelical worship through one of its main characters, who rises to the status of worship leader in his small Korean evangelical church. Explaining to his adoring fans after a service one day, he shows them the tricks of the trade with his guitar: "And if you use D minor, you can really feel the Holy Spirit." Danny Cho replaced the dethroned worship leader whose violent outburst revealed he was unfit for church leadership. Though Cho is equally unqualified to serve as a spiritual leader, he is able to deceive the congregation through his musical talent and seemingly humble charisma. Though his spiritual fraudulence is only one of many narratives about Danny's life, the scene portrays the ease with which the affective nature of evangelical worship promotes insincerity and manipulation.

In real life, former evangelicals who found community and meaning in these churches feel a deep sense of betrayal. This is especially true for people who donated extensive time and talent in hope of being seen as a valuable member of the community, only to be disappointed by how easily their work was exploited and their own moral intuitions subverted by authoritarian forces.

Performing in her church's music ministry was always the center of Grace's identity. Like a lot of young evangelicals in the 1990s and early 2000s, Grace's entire sense of self was shaped by her church community. "My best friends were there. I had individuals in the church community who had known me since I was born. I had people who were, like, adopted grandparents, adopted aunts and uncles." From a young age, Grace, who participated in an After Purity Project interview, was very involved in church ministry. By the age of fourteen, she was a worship leader at her church, a substantial responsibility that she willingly embraced. As a singer, Grace loved performing, but she also internalized the virtue of modesty around the use of her voice. "I felt guilty for thinking about those as things that I wanted from my life, because that was not doing God's work or helping people. It wasn't to be famous and rich, just to do something that I loved.²"

As an adult, Grace attended a large, well-known Pentecostal church in Virginia with a celebrity pastor, the kind that draws large numbers because of its ability to make people feel culturally savvy and upwardly mobile. While mega-churches that were designed to attract "the unchurched" entered the American religious landscape in the 1970s, by the 1990s and 2000s, various adaptations of the seeker-friendly church had become a global phenomenon, especially among people under the age of forty.³ It is unsurprising, then, that Grace was attracted to a church in her adulthood that carefully curated musical performances and utilized the gravitational pull of celebrity. But instead of offering her opportunities to share her talent and enjoy the spotlight, the church's young adult ministry had other ideas.

In large evangelical churches, young adult ministries function as marriage incubators. In some cases, these are informal networks that allow young people to develop friendships or romantic relationships, allowing them to push the boundaries of purity culture if they so choose. But in a larger church, in which ministries are divided by age group, people in their twenties can be fairly certain of finding a dating culture pushing them toward marriage. At Grace's church, the process was formalized so that young couples "getting serious" were expected to work with a couples' mentor, an older married couple in the church who provided advice and oversight in the hopes of getting the couple to the altar before sexual desire derailed them.

As she began a relationship with a man in her church group, Grace began to feel the overreach of purity culture into her life. Both she and her boyfriend were very interested in sex but also felt obligated to abstain for their church community. But the tension between her sexual desire and her sense of obligation started shifting Grace away from purity ideology.

Soon, however, Grace began to catch her partner in little lies, revealing a pattern of deception. She asked a family member to run a background check on him and discovered that he had lied about several significant parts of his life. The couple's mentor had similar suspicions, but never confronted the boyfriend, leaving Grace to do the heavy lifting of exposing him to their entire church and ending their relationship.

After the breakup, Grace discovered was that while her desire to marry this man had faded upon revelations of his fraud, her sexual desire for him did not. After attending a wedding of mutual friends together, Grace decided she wanted to have sex. Knowing she no longer felt an emotional connection to him, nor an obligation to purity culture, she declared, "Fuck it, let's go, get some condoms and whatever." It was the first time for them both, and it wasn't a great experience, Grace told me. But for her it was a choice grounded in her sexual desire that allowed her to actively participate in shattering the sacred fairy tale that had held her captive for so long. "You know, like, here I am, I met this guy in church just how you're supposed to. You know, we've been trying to do it God's way. And it turns out he was a fraud."

Like many of the former evangelicals I interviewed, Grace expressed grief over a significant amount of loss: the tight-knit community of her childhood, a sense of belonging and purpose, and the romantic aspirations of true love. Her story is a common one among people who identify as ex-vangelical. Though leaving one's faith tradition or community is a long and storied human experience, the phenomenon of being an ex-vangelical is noteworthy because it has become an identity in and of itself.

More than a hundred people submitted demographic data to the After Purity Project, including descriptions of their former and current religious and/or spiritual affiliations and identities. Using that information, I created a tentative set of categories around these responses, tentative because the ex-vangelical moniker, as Blake Chastain explains, "can be a liminal space. It isn't meant to describe all of you."[4] Given that so many former evangelicals never had the option for spiritual experimentation, the "ex" aspect of ex-vangelicalism remains open-ended.

For some, being an ex-vangelical does not mean abandoning Christianity at all, though its liminality allows those who remain to blur the boundaries between Christian beliefs and those of other religious practices, even if the ex-vangelical maintains a formal affiliation with a Christian denomination. In White evangelicalism, racial justice is not a religious virtue. This became evident to Amanda, who describes herself as Black and biracial. After eight Black church members and their pastor in Charleston, South Carolina, were murdered by an unrepentant White supremacist, her White pastor discussed the incident in the context of forgiveness. She was horrified. She had previously noted that same pastor's alarmist response to the legalization of gay marriage. For ex-vangelicals, social issues such as racism, homophobia, and misogyny are key factors that influenced their departure from the evangelical community. For Amanda, her distress over evangelical attitudes meant researching other church traditions that held more progressive views on these issues. At the time of our interview, in 2020, she was expressing interest in becoming more involved in the Episcopal Church.

Amanda falls into the first category I developed: the *Affiliated Christian* category, which I use for people who wish to remain in a Christianity community after leaving evangelicalism. All descriptions of the categories I've developed reflect participants' comments at the time of our interview. Given the dynamic nature of Chastain's definition, I do not assume these responses reflect participants' current state of belief or unbelief. Many of my research participants found other Christian denominations a suitable substitute, including the Episcopalian Church, the Presbyterian Church (USA), the Anglican Church of Canada, and the United Methodist Church. But even more identified themselves as Christian outside traditional denominational structures altogether. In the 1970s, many evangelical churches began branding themselves as nondenominational, even if they had a denominational connection. Marketing research has indicated that potential churchgoers in the late twentieth century had little concern for theological traditions such as Calvinism or Wesleyanism and had even less interest in a traditional church experience. So, evangelicals, such as those who founded Willow Creek Church, considered the first of this kind, strategically set about designing seeker-friendly churches that accommodated the needs of the "unchurched," transforming them into consumers on a quest for personalized spiritual satisfaction that included the acceptance, if not celebration, of a prosperous lifestyle.[5]

The second category I developed for former evangelicals is heavily indebted to this history: *Unaffiliated Christian*. These are people who used adjectives such as *progressive, deconstructing, universalist, contemplative, mystical*, and *spiritual* in their self-descriptions. They are informed by late twentieth-century trends in spirituality that saw individuals crafting a religious identity outside formal church structures. This group is the most comfortable describing themselves as participating in the deconstruction process, which is the practice of evaluating Christian beliefs in light of changing norms and personal identity. These are people who may remain active in a Christian community yet allow themselves to shun the label. Others enjoy being in a whole community dedicated to asking theological questions that were never permitted in their former church context.

Ex-vangelicalism is best described as a spectrum that extends through and beyond Christianity. At the nexus of through and beyond is the category I call *Christian Hybrid*. These are people whose self-descriptions indicate a connection to Christian spirituality *and* to something that is not Christianity, such as another religious or spiritual tradition or a social justice movement. They include college students who take courses on Buddhism and discover a new set of spiritual practices, LGBTQIA folks who discover a feminist spirituality that offers healing from homophobia and misogyny, and White people who develop an understanding of how Christianity promotes their own White racial privilege. Christian hybridism indicates that many ex-vangelicals seek to lower the exclusionary boundaries of their former communities. This often means becoming less concerned with what is and is not "Christian." Rather, the search is to determine what is just, inclusive, and allows all people to live authentic lives.

The fourth category I created, *Rejectionists*, includes people who have decided to leave or fervently reject Christianity as a whole. For those who leave and never look back, the moral expectations of purity culture, including its innate homophobia and misogyny, played an outsize role in their leaving. Struggling with socio-sexual development, many ex-vangelicals seek out the resources their churches and families did not provide. Robust conversations about LGBTQIA inclusion, along with a severe yet careful critique of complementarian theology, are fostered at various degrees of separation from evangelicalism, including from within. In some ways, the markers of ex-vangelical belief are those of the evangelicals, but in contradistinction. But to portray ex-vangelicals as mirror images of their former selves with different sociopolitical objectives fails to help us understand why people leave evangelicalism for another tradition, or for none at all.

Because the line between Hybrid Christian and Non-Christian is difficult to determine, I created another category I simply call *Uncertain*. Here, I include the possibility that one can still be Christian in habits of thought and belief yet feel unsettled by their continued proximity to these. This could be because people are in a family and work situation that makes it difficult to leave their Christian community and are required to continue to perform the functions associated with their obligations, including remaining in a marriage despite needing to leave (or having just left) and remaining employed in a particular job, such as a church worker. The support system that evangelicals offer their members is extensive, especially within more tight-knit communities. In some cases, the dependency is solicited in order to keep people committed and giving of their time, labor, and money. As Chastain noted above, leaving a church can sometimes means leaving your entire social network. A high-investment church demands high boundaries between "us" and "them," so when an individual or family leaves, the impact for them is palpable, if not traumatic. For those who depend on church friends for car pools, emotional support, or a quickly activated meal-train, those resources can be rescinded very quickly when they leave a high-investment church. This is why many ex-vangelicals find themselves drawn to conversations about religious or spiritual trauma. Some, including several of my interviewees, followed this need into new careers focused on understanding the ex-vangelical experience and helping people heal from the grief and loss that accompany it.

Stories of people leaving White evangelicalism have become especially prominent in the last decade as the youth of the 1990s and early 2000s became adults. Evangelical churches became more deeply entrenched in anti-LGBTQIA ideologies and demanded allegiance to political conservativism. White evangelicals in the US unquestioningly threw their support behind Donald Trump and looked askance at the racial reckoning led by Black Lives Matter. Some found evangelical theology lacking in substance, while others recognized the cruelty of theological teachings of sin and obedience. Still others experienced ostracization and condemnation because of their gender or sexual or racial identity. The After Purity Project has gathered just one set of data that demonstrates the significant role that purity culture is playing in the ex-vangelical exodus.

My interviewees cited several reasons for leaving behind the adverse experiences of purity culture teachings. But first it's important to understand how they experienced their White evangelical communities and families of origin as a set of tight-knit relationships in which the boundaries between church and world were safe and stifling all at once. Jessica, who today describes herself as nonreligious, reflected fondly on the church community of her adolescence,

> I think back to those times and it was like built-in friends and, you know, it was like the kids you went to church with, and you became very close because you were around them constantly. And I felt like it was a community that I could at least somewhat like be myself around a lot of the other girls, and we have very close friendships. So those were definitely the good parts that I look back on fondly.[6]

Evangelical communities are very good at developing the tight-knit bonds that offer personal relationships laden with spiritual significance. At the age of sixteen, however, Jessica discovered the boundary that policed relationships between insiders and outsiders to the evangelical faith. Her first experience in the heteronormative dating world was outside her church community. Adult members shared their discomfort with her mom, who also disapproved of the relationship. As a result, Jessica lost all the interpersonal support she had come to depend on. "It just became something that I couldn't talk to her or anyone about. The relationship wasn't healthy either. [. . .] But regardless of that, I felt like I had no one to talk to about it. So it kind of set me up for failure almost because I was a sixteen-year-old girl that had her first relationship and didn't really have anywhere to go to vent or discuss." While Jessica very much enjoyed the close and caring relationships she found within her church, she found that dating someone of the opposite sex outside the fold and crossing certain boundaries meant relinquishing her right to that care.

Evangelical communities are often constructed around an all-or-nothing sensibility. Katy called herself "an official I don't know person" when I asked her to describe her current religious/spiritual beliefs. Reflecting on her evangelical past, she referred to it as all-consuming.

> Extracting yourself from evangelicalism takes so much work, you know, because it's your whole life. I went to a private Christian school. I went to a church. I was in church [. . .] every like almost every day, you know, from the ages of, like, five until I was twenty years old, you know. It's like every aspect of your life is enveloped in Christianity, because that's just the evangelical way. You know, I didn't even have friends that weren't Christians until I got to college.[7]

When Katy tries to explain evangelicalism to people who did not grow up in the church, she struggles to describe the depth of her commitment and how her early life was shaped by a military strictness that she learned to exert upon herself. Her decision not to have sex before marriage wasn't about future relationships or her own well-being but about maintaining a good relationship with God and with her community. She understood her commitment to purity as a heavy obligation to both. "It's me making an active decision to, like, have a relationship with God, have a relationship with my church, be that kind of person in my community. It's so further reaching than just my body and my choices."

Roseanne grew up in the church her mother attended her entire life, where she met and married Roseanne's father. Roseanne described it as a bubble in San Francisco's Bay Area, where she was separated from the complicated questions raised by the presence of a prominent and diverse LGBTQIA community. She described her teenage faith as zealous, once wondering if her father was going to hell because he drank a glass of wine on a work trip. Her faith commitment extended to her political commitments, believing that as a Christian she could only support Republican candidates because of their pro-life platform and opposition to gay marriage. She recounted a journal entry from November 28, 2004, in which she praised God for the reelection of George W. Bush.

As an adult, Roseanne conducts thought experiments around her religious belief as a way to determine her spiritual orientation.

> Right now I'm experimenting with not being a Christian, with not calling myself a Christian. I experimented with not believing in God, but then I felt really upset when I thought about that, if there was no God. So, I believe in God. [. . .] Like as of like last week I am not a Christian. It's been a long process since I was eighteen. [. . .] I'm almost thirty-four, but just the last few months just realized, like, if you just tweak your view a little bit, Christianity really seems like a cult. And so that's how I am right now, just kind of pulling myself out of it. And then I think eventually I will try to see the good, but right now I'm feeling like there was more harm than good even for me in the world.[8]

Roseanne is one of the reasons I created the *Uncertain* category. She is not the only person I spoke with who refused to reconstruct the strict boundaries that shaped her earliest Christian identity. The possibility of being agnostic and a Christian, of being Christian and another faith tradition, or leaving altogether—Roseanne wants all of those options on the table and the time to discern which feels most authentic for her. This is characteristic of many ex-vangelicals for whom leaving the faith is just one small step in a much longer passage through uncertainty. It's not simply about de-converting, losing one's faith, or choosing another path. It's about rearranging your entire understanding of what it means to construct and hold a belief system. Many of my interviewees were raised in environments where raising theological questions and doubts were considered a spiritual weakness or even sinful. Overwhelmingly, ex-evangelicals believe that faith and doubt are inseparable, which is a concept that thrives in other theological contexts and even some more intellectually focused evangelical circles. But on the whole, obedience and conformity in White evangelical communities mean that doubts and questions are out of bounds, along with those who have them.

Tina, who attends a Methodist church, also grew up in a family-centric evangelical church. Her grandfather was a preacher in the Independent Fundamental Baptist Church, an unaffiliated group of churches that promotes cultural separatism through homeschooling and Christian education. For Tina, getting from school to church meant simply walking across the parking lot.

> I kind of joke with people that if I wasn't at school, I was at church, but they were the same building. And then if I wasn't at church, I was at school, and if I wasn't in any one of those places, I was at another church and or school that was associated with a church and or school.[9]

Even as an adult, Tina and her husband were deeply invested in church life, serving in numerous volunteer positions. However, she had learned that church was not a place to bring painful elements of her life. "Everything is rose-colored glasses and hunky-dory," she said, so when her husband had significant struggles with his mental health and eventually divorced her, she did not seek or find solace within her church. Today she attends a Methodist church where she sings on the praise team, and her boyfriend, who has also deconstructed his evangelical faith, finds many opportunities for social justice work.

I was surprised at how many of my research participants fall into the *Affiliated Christian* category. This is important, especially for those who associate deconstruction with a sledgehammer approach to Christianity. The presence of ex-vangelicals in non-evangelical Christian churches shows us that, for many, the process of deconstruction is not about undermining Christian community, nor is about building new boundaries separating insiders and outsiders. Deconstruction, when understood as both a personal and structural shift, is committed to dismantling ideologies of supremacy culture that elevate Christianity as the only true faith tradition. For those unable to acknowledge the problem of Christian supremacy, deconstruction feels like a threat of extinction. Fortunately, there are numerous Christian communities that do not invest in theological exceptionalism, where former evangelicals can participate in Christian community and worship without having to divide their world in two.

Religious communities with high boundaries are often defined by the high investment they demand of members. For Keely, who now describes herself as agnostic, this meant planning on dying at the age of twenty-five. She was all in as a teenager, internalizing the Calvinist doctrine that humans suffer from total depravity and crying herself to sleep many nights because she knew she would never measure up.

> I remember feeling constantly, like, I wasn't enough. I just couldn't do it. I wasn't enough. I was constantly bad. I'm a poor Christian, even though things were tough for me, you know, like just really like they are as a teenager. It's not easy. I was just, like, well, I can't complain because God doesn't like a complainer.[10]

As a young person who was theologically driven, Keely desired to become a pastor, but women are not permitted in her Christian Reformed denomination. She felt that her commitment and passion were overlooked by her church because she was a young woman, and struggled with the disconnect between who she wanted to be and who she was expected to be.

But in the decade of the mass shooting at Columbine High School, where two students killed thirteen people, one victim became a role model for young evangelicals. In the memoir *She Said Yes*, Cassie Bernall is portrayed by her mother as a Christian martyr. According to the story, the shooters were asking Christian students to identify themselves. Those who did were shot dead. The fabricated version of this story claims that, despite the threat to her life Cassie still responded yes. She was among the thirteen killed that day, but the martyrdom myth that emerged after was not an accurate account of what happened.[11]

Influenced by martyr narratives such as Cassie's, Keely realized that while she couldn't be an ordained pastor, she could become a missionary and a martyr to her faith.

> One day I'm going to be a martyr and I'll show the world that, you know, that I really love God. I had this big belief that that's what my calling was in life. I would be dead by the age of twenty-five. And so it's interesting because I thought that that was unique to me, and hearing other stories of people who have deconstructed, it's a common narrative, particularly for women. But that is one thing that, you know, coming to learn and be compassionate towards myself, like, that's the only way I saw being able to be Christian. [. . .] Looking back now, it feels like quite an abusive relationship with God.

To this day, Keely is unable to share important details of her life with her parents, who would find her decisions unacceptable. They still don't know that she and her husband lived together for two years before marrying. Nor has she been able to tell them that she is no longer a Christian. Like many other ex-vangelicals, Keely must behave around evangelicals as if the expectations of her parents' faith are still intact for her. To threaten the boundary between belief and unbelief means confronting her parents with the harm she experienced in their high-investment church community.

Rose, an Affiliated Christian now in the Episcopal Church, also struggled with the restrictions placed on her because of her gender. As an evangelical, Rose was often the only woman in the campus apologetics club debating theological issues and sharpening her critical thinking skills. In college she attended a prominent evangelical church affiliated with the Southern Baptist Convention. Her pastor, J. D. Greear, would eventually serve as the denomination's president at the height of the SBC clergy sex-abuse scandal. At first, Rose found the complementarian theology of the SBC intriguing. "I became really sympathetic to complementarianism, and I think it was because I had just, like, constantly found myself in roles where I was having to take responsibility, and the idea of getting married to a man who would just take care of stuff actually sounded really nice. I was like, okay—so complementarianism seems great."[12]

Complementarian theology has been SBC orthodoxy since the early 1980s. Though church leaders claim it is a "biblical" (and therefore the only allowable) understanding of gender, the model is derived from nineteenth-century gender roles fashioned by White Protestants to resemble Victorian culture in England. As more White families achieved middle-class status and no longer depended on a domestic economy that both men and women participated in, Victorian-era Protestants felt conflicted about their growing wealth, which they associated with an immodest lifestyle. But instead of curbing financial growth, they developed an idealized family model that would permit men to do the unsavory work of business and politics. The model requires their wives to maintain a home that serves as a domestic sanctuary. "The angel in the house" was a domestic priestess charged with her children's spiritual formation and with maintaining her own moral superiority. Though centuries of Christian history denounced women as the sex willing and able to use sexual allure to beckon men into sin, Victorian gender roles fully reversed this view.[13]

Because men had to deal with unsavory work such as finance and politics that required them to walk a moral tightrope, nineteenth-century gender roles asserted that they were meant for this work because they were less virtuous than women, therefore an eventual fall from grace was expected. But when those men returned from the rough-and-tumble worlds of banking, industry, and politics, they would be restored to their moral core by their home life, carefully curated by their wives' ability to maintain their own moral fortitude. Though it was only accessible to the most wealthy, since working-class and even many middle-class women had to work to support their family, this model of domestic life was promoted in women's magazines, church sermons, and advertisements as the ideal family arrangement for White people seeking upper-class status while maintaining the appearance of moral respectability.

Among the virtues ascribed to nineteenth-century Victorian-era women were domesticity (women's work and authority is limited to the home), religious piety (women were naturally more religious than man), submission (women were to submit to their husband's authority), and purity (women are naturally uninterested in sex beyond the purpose of motherhood). When the conservative takeover in the SBC began in the late 1970s, it was in response to the growing popularity of evangelical feminism. The leaders of the takeover assumed Victorian-era gender roles as biblical, even though they were more prominently portrayed in nineteenth-century women's magazines than in people's actual lives. Constructed as a White supremacist, patriarchal system, the Victorian family structure does not sit well in the late twentieth century as roiling debates over women's roles in the church demonstrate. Among Southern Baptists, complementarian theology—the belief that men and women have equally important yet distinct roles—means that women are not allowed to be in authority over men, which severely limits the work that women can do in the church without drawing opposition.

Though initially intrigued by complementarian theology, Rose did not imagine herself being satisfied with the life it would require of her. She was an intellectual engaged in deep theological inquiry. After taking some religious studies courses in college, she wondered if she was being called to the pastorate. But that did not square with complementarian theology. When she reflects on it now, she realizes this was the beginning of her deconstruction.

> I was in this period of wondering, like, am I supposed to be a linguistics professor? Am I supposed to be a pastor? Or am I supposed to be a religion professor? Like what what's going on? And the gender stuff kind of started to unravel, and I think that laid the groundwork for the purity culture stuff also unraveling and just evangelicalism in general unraveling.

But even as Rose found the freedom to ask theological questions, any inquiry into her beliefs about not having sex before marriage felt insurmountable. She had panic attacks while researching her questions about sex. It was what she called an "untouchable doctrine," a physical boundary so strong she could not even approach it with questions. In our interview, she said that doubting purity culture brought her to tears in a way that her doubts around more traditional theological claims did not.

As a man, Joel was allowed to serve in church leadership, which he did for several years as a youth minister. Though not much younger than himself, the young people in his church learned from him that they needed to stay as far away from sex as possible. Failure to do so would result in guilt, the inevitable result of experiencing any degree of sexual pleasure outside of marriage. Now Joel says he deeply regrets teaching teenagers such harmful views. But while he was teaching others, the lessons were embedding themselves in his own body. Just two years after marrying his high school girlfriend in front of a large audience that included numerous admiring teenagers, he began to doubt everything. Though leaving his church was a rigorous and painful task that he still feels the impact of, he says leaving behind the purity culture was even more arduous. For Joel, who falls into the non-Christian category of ex-vangelicals, there is no distinction between evangelicalism and purity culture, and therefore no way to deconstruct evangelicalism without also disassembling purity culture. But as he's reflected on his own deconstruction experience, Joel has realized that questioning and rejecting his old belief system was not the same thing as reprogramming his body around sexual desire. The physical adjustment to life outside of purity culture was more jarring than the intellectual adjustment of leaving evangelical theology behind.[14]

Some of my research participants have been able to build community with other ex-vangelicals, though they have come to realize how easily the exclusionary boundaries they fled can be replicated. Gabe, whom I categorize as an Unaffiliated Christian and who describes himself as post-evangelical, joined a small group of other ex-vangelicals who meet regularly outside of church spaces. As an Asian American and Chinese immigrant, he is the only person of color in the group. But what they all have in common is the experience of being deeply hurt by a former evangelical community.

During our conversation Gabe revealed to me that he'd recently been renegotiating his relationship with the all-White group after a shooting in Atlanta, Georgia, that left eight people dead, including six Asian women. The growing anti-Asian hostility in the nation had begun to shift his sense of self in all-White spaces, which became readily evident when no one brought up the shooting at their meeting. A violent incident that completely reoriented his life was not even on the radar of others in his group. Raising the topic with them only furthered his feelings of being unseen and unheard.[15]

The shooting Gabe referred to was a significant escalation of anti-Asian violence that had begun during the COVID-19 pandemic. Twenty-one-year-old Robert Aaron Long, a White man, traveled to three different spas in Atlanta targeting employees at each. Authorities were not convinced that the shooter was driven by anti-Asian racism because the explanation he gave while in custody did not include a discussion of race. Given that the police officers did not acknowledge how unconscious bias against Asian women informed Long's actions, they accepted his explanation for his actions. According to reports from his interview with police, Long said he was attempting to rid himself of the object of his sexual temptation.[16]

Long was an active member of Southern Baptist Church who had previously been sent to a treatment center for sexual addiction. As a Christian who believed his sexual desires and practices were in contradiction to his faith, Long told police that he was tortured by sexual temptations and had paid for sexual services at spas, including one he targeted during his shooting rampage. Given that his Christian beliefs would not allow him to accept his sexual practices as part of the normal spectrum of human sexuality, he projected his ire onto the women he had come to see as objects of his sexual desire. When his parents kicked him out of the house for his sex addiction, his distress drove him to eliminate the people he felt were responsible for his lust: Asian and Asian American women.[17]

Gabe's experience in his ex-vangelical group demonstrates the color-evasive racism that permeates White evangelical communities. Though my research participants were overwhelmingly White, the few people of color I interviewed mentioned experiences of racism within their former churches. With the growing awareness of police aggression and a justice system biased against African Americans, Black evangelicals in predominantly White churches discovered that these issues did not resonate on the same scale with their fellow White parishioners. As mentioned earlier, Amanda listened to her White pastor prioritize forgiveness from the pulpit after a self-proclaimed

White supremacist murdered eight Black people at Bible study in Charleston, South Carolina. Before he did so, the shooter announced, "You rape our women," invoking a century of fears about Black men's sexuality (though most of the victims of the shooting were women).[18] Amanda told me she was "horrified" that her pastor's remarks did not address the racist violence of the incident. Coupled with the pastor's criticisms of Barack Obama and gay marriage, she realized how deeply her Christian faith had been informed by White supremacist ideology, which she now understood reinforces forgiveness over justice and the status quo over inclusion and diversity.

Mikayla had a similar experience a few years earlier after another high-profile shooting. An African American therapist who describes herself as "not an evangelical anymore, but I wouldn't say I'm an atheist, somewhere in-between," she is another example of the *Uncertain* category and the liminality of the ex-vangelical experience, which requires us to see the category as transitory. Mikayla and her family attended a majority-White evangelical church in Sanford, Florida, where, in 2012, a young Black man on his way home from the store was confronted by a self-appointed neighborhood watchman. They had a physical altercation and the young Black man was shot and killed. Within a year, George Zimmerman would be acquitted for the murder of Trayvon Martin because of Florida's "Stand Your Ground" law, which allows private citizens to use excessive force if they believe they are or their property is at risk.

As a teenager living ten minutes from where Martin was shot and killed, Mikayla found that his death instigated a new level of caution and awareness about the risk of being Black in America. At first her church made a show of support for those who were grieving, taking part in high-profile events in which church members could be perceived, she said, as "great Christians, rallying behind our city to bring unity." But even early on, Mikayla felt the church's response was shallow and ignored the difficult questions the killing raised about policing and "Stand Your Ground" laws.

But even that response disappeared when Zimmerman was acquitted of murdering Martin. Within her church, White members began speaking about Martin as if he had been responsible for his own death, said Mikayla, that "he should have complied and listened," completely disregarding other facts of the case, like Martin's age (he was seventeen) and Zimmerman's assumptions about community policing. After the acquittal, Mikayla realized that she had been trained into silence, especially when it meant contradicting White people and authority figures. She and her sister had always been lauded by fellow parishioners for being "so well mannered," but as she started speaking up about Black people's experiences of racism, those compliments faded.

Two years later, Michael Brown was shot and killed by a White police officer in Ferguson, Missouri. The protests that started two years earlier grew following Brown's murder. By this time, Mikayla noticed that neither her fellow church members nor the church leadership had expressed any concern for police brutality toward African Americans. She listened as White evangelicals in her church made racist jokes and asserted that Brown had deserved to die. The final straw for Mikayla (who stayed at the church longer than others in her family) was after the death of police officers in Dallas, Texas. The next Sunday her pastor preached a sermon that included a Power-Point slide reading "Blue Lives Matter" and included photos of all the police families in the church. Mikayla shared her frustration with a trusted mentor, an older, White woman in the congregation who did not understand racism beyond personal behaviors and attitudes. But Mikayla trusted her mentor, who shared that, even as a White person, she had learned to distrust other White people at a young age, while experiencing kindness from Black people. But, as Mikayla learned, that didn't necessarily translate into her mentor understanding how racism works. Her mentor explained to Mikayla that she was "color-blind," meaning that she did not believe that she made judgments about people due to their race.[19] Furthermore, she was married to a police officer. For Mikayla, this meant that good White Christians could say "Blue Lives Matter" without understanding it as a reactionary statement against Black Lives Matter and the ongoing racial reckoning prompted by police violence. In describing this moment to me, Mikayla reflected on how she struggled to understand the inability of White people who cared about her to completely dismiss racism as a system of oppression. She knew the people in her church did not understand her experience as a young Black woman living through a season of anti-Black violence. When she saw the Blue Lives Matter slide, she knew they would never understand the extensive harm of structural racism. Four months later, she left the White evangelical church for good.

CHAPTER FOUR

CONSTRUCTING THE MYTH OF WHITE RACIAL IDENTITY

THE AFTER PURITY PROJECT was not designed or publicized as a project about racial identity. Most of my research participants did not speak about the topic in our interviews. It's notable that those who did were the few people of color who contributed their stories. This alone tells us a great deal about White racial identity: it often remains invisible and therefore unquestioned as representing normative experiences. There are many reasons why I didn't design the project around the intersection of sexual purity and racial identity, but mostly I was concerned the combination of the two would scare White people away and tokenize people of color. I wanted to allow potential participants the greatest amount of agency in self-selecting into the study. But even this assumes the invisibility of my own racial identity, something that became clear as I watched who signed up—people who were a lot like me: well-educated, professional White women. The first group interview (an experimental stage of the project) was composed of all White women with or working toward PhDs in fields related to my own. After struggling with some of my own racial anxiety about my inability to attract participants of color, I was gently prompted to consider why non-White women might not be drawn to research on sexual purity conducted by a White woman. Within communities of color, sexual purity is a concept that is understood as intersectional; it is as much about race as it is about sexuality. And anyone who has historical memory recognizes that sexual purity has been associated with racial purity under deeply violent circumstances. Because Whiteness functions as it does, as normative and invisible to those who embody it, discussions of sexual purity in White communities can remain artificially isolated from other powerful ideologies like White supremacy.

All of my research participants did answer an opened-ended survey prompt: How would you describe your racial/ethnic identity? Given that my respondents were overwhelmingly White women, I was interested to see the different ways they each named their Whiteness. Of the ninety-four people who completed the survey, seventy responded "White," fourteen responded "Caucasian," and four responded "White/ Caucasian." Several others responded "White" and something else, adding the nuances of their ethnic identity. These included "White/ European," "White with Scottish/German roots," "White (first-gen Eastern European)," "multi-ethnic, White-passing," "White (Mennonite)," "White, Jewish, Baltic, Nordic, French," "White Appalachian," "Jewish/White," "White/non-Hispanic," and "biracial (White, Mexican/Latinx)."

These responses indicate something notable about White racial identity. While "Whiteness" has been constructed (by scientists, legal systems, medical systems, and even insurance providers) to designate superior groups, there has never been any consensus around who exactly qualifies as white. In the early twentieth century, US laws granting citizenship remained governed by the 1790 Naturalization Act, which included the term "free White persons," creating a racial requirement for citizenship. Also in that era, the scientific study of race, later known as the eugenics movement, claimed that genetic coding proved racial superiority and inferiority.

Though there was never a stable consensus, White racial identity, also referred to by the invented category *Caucasian*, was shaped by a politics of exclusion, holding a place only for those designated genetically or socially superior. As European immigrant groups assimilated into US culture (if they were able to do so based on their physical appearance and place of origin) by being recognized by other White people as White, they were considered such. As flimsy as this definition may seem, in the early twentieth century, it was used by the US Supreme Court, which had the responsibility of determining who was White and was therefore eligible to become a citizen of the United States.

Whiteness informs cultural norms and religious expectations around sexual purity, particularly the meanings and representations of White womanhood. Though today Whiteness is most unique as an invisible racial category, in earlier eras when racist norms sought to maintain the boundary between Black and White, the presumed sexual purity of White womanhood served as a powerful boundary marker. In the United States, racial categories formed around laws and cultural norms that mandated the separation of the races. Though these norms have shifted in the post–civil rights era, this country has never fully examined how fears of race mixing have impacted our cultural imagination and informed our habits. As a campaign started in the context of White evangelicalism, purity culture continues to exploit these fears without drawing attention to the underlying racism that permeates how Americans meet, mate, and settle into long-term relationships.

In order to understand the use and meanings of White womanhood in the development of sexual purity ideology, we need to unpack the creation of White racial identity as a category shaped first to dominate all other groups and, second, to obscure itself in order to maintain that dominance.

Racial identity formation is premised on the understanding that all racial identities are social constructs. When I explain this to my students, I tell them that we first have to understand that race is not a biological reality. Though racial categorization (and stereotyping) is sometimes based on biological markers, race is much more than the phenotypical features we exhibit. To say that race is a social construct is to understand that race is the result of processes by which we attach meaning to those features and associate them with entire groups. As this chapter demonstrates, those processes are historical, legal, religious, and scientific.

In the era of European colonial expansion, White racial identity emerged as the racialization of spiritual superiority: populations identified as Christian were "saved" from barbarism and capable of reaching the highest mark of human civilization. The colonization of non-Christian territories by European Christian nations was justified by the Catholic Church's Doctrine of Discovery, which obligated Euro-Christian civilizations to explore, conquer, and exploit non-European peoples. Even when scientific inquiry began to replace religion as the source of all important knowledge, it did not challenge the colonial logics of European supremacy. Scientists of the eighteenth and nineteenth centuries only reaffirmed these claims with rudimentary (and inaccurate) biological data.

The origin of the racial category Caucasian is especially helpful for understanding how early race scientists used both religious myth and biological data to construct a racial category that naturalized Euro-Christian superiority. Even today, the classification "Caucasian" remains relatively uncontroversial, despite its lack of scientific veracity and the use of the concept to consolidate White racial power in the early twentieth century.

In the earliest iterations of his work on Caucasians, the eighteenth-century German scientist Johann Friedrich Blumenbach drew upon the biblical story of Noah and his three sons, Shem, Ham, and Japheth. After the Great Flood, Noah's ancestors spread in three directions, which some readers concluded was an indication of the creation of three racial groups. Though later readers, especially those seeking to justify the enslavement of Africans, would claim that the story marked Ham's descendants as cursed to slavery, Blumenbach initially submitted that each brother was an ancestor to the three branches of the Caucasian tree: the Hamites of the Nile Valley and Ethiopian highlands; the S(h)emites, who include the Israelites and Arabs; and the most dominant, due to their ability to conquer the more "passive" races, the Japhethites, also known as the Aryans.[1]

Blumenbach wanted to understand if and why skulls from the same geographical region were similar in size and shape. Typological analysis allowed him to begin developing a racial schema that included five categories: Malay, Ethiopian, Mongolian, American (Indigenous), and European. When his research turned to the study of skulls from the Caucasus region, Blumenbach was enamored, a fascination that left an indelible mark on our racial categories. Some stories suggest that his fondness for Caucasian women biased his assessment of the regional skull, which he came to revere as the most beautiful and perfect of his collection. This, and his favoring of the Caucasian people as a whole, led him to conclude that all Europeans had originated from the region. Blumenbach would eventually refine the Caucasian category to include only groups of European descent, and though it would become just one of dozens of ways to name White racial identity throughout 150 years of racial science, the single constant was the claimed superiority of the Caucasian category.[2]

By the publication of his book *On the Natural Varieties of Mankind* in 1775, Blumenbach had replaced the category "European" with "Caucasian." He described the Caucasian race as the high-water mark of human civilization.

> The leading nations of the world who have reached the highest state of civilization belong to this race. It is from this that the Caucasian race has been called the "active race," while others, embracing the uncivilized or half-civilized peoples, have been termed the "passive races."[3]

Despite the lack of scientific evidence and the long-standing debate among anthropologists over what exactly constituted a racial category, the word *Caucasian* stuck. We use it today with limited controversy to name people of European descent. But at the height of scientific racism, being identified as Caucasian (as opposed to Celtic, Nordic, Anglo, or one of the other thirty to forty categories created to designate what we now call White) held a significant amount of cultural and legal currency.

In the early twentieth century, fears of new immigrants and race mixing were easily justified by the new and improved race science that could now identify heritable traits and determine what were then thought of as inferior or superior genetic compositions. In this era, both legal and scientific fields were concerned with identifying Whiteness as a trait closely linked to the rights of citizenship. In the 1920s, the US Supreme Court began using its power to determine who was and was not White, or, more specifically, Caucasian and could therefore be granted citizenship. The racial landscape at this time was still dominated by the color line that separated Black and White. Chinese, Mexican, Italian, Greek, and Eastern European immigrants disrupted this binary, creating an urgency for determining an individual's racial status.

Takao Ozawa was an immigrant whose family had assimilated seamlessly into the United States. They lived in an entirely White world, practiced the Christian faith, and only spoke English. The pressure for immigrants to relinquish any and all markers of their previous national identity, cultural norms, and values was immense. Ozawa learned the rules of fitting in and with his family became a model citizen. But race science dictated that Ozawa could never fully fit in because of the racial genetics that categorized him as Mongolian.[4]

A counternarrative within sociological analysis and popular culture in the earliest decades of the twentieth century used the metaphor of the melting pot, which portrays assimilation as a process of blending the cultures of a variety of immigrants into a whole. This was possible for European immigrants whose genetic traits identified them as White and therefore capable of adapting to an "American" way of life. But if your genetic expression was too distinct from (i.e., inferior to) that of "the average White American," the courts would ultimately find that you could not assimilate and therefore would not be granted citizenship. And this is precisely what happened to Ozawa. In 1922, he petitioned for citizenship but was denied because the court determined Ozawa was not White.

The implications of Ozawa's denial were catastrophic for Asian Americans already granted citizenship. Not only was their citizenship revoked, but landowning laws in states like California required citizenship in order to own land. The thousands of Japanese and other Asian Americans who made their living farming their own land lost their livelihood and now had to fear deportation and family separation, along with the anti-Asian violence that had gone unchecked for decades.

Three year earlier another immigrant, Bhagat Singh Thind, from Punjab, India, would petition for citizenship. Thind was well-educated, deeply religious, and had fought for the United States in World War I. He initially received approval for naturalization, but in 1922 the Supreme Court reviewed his case in light of the Ozawa findings. In preparing his defense, Thind and his lawyers built an argument that rested on the scientific accuracy of the racial sciences. Though Ozawa was Mongolian and therefore could not be granted citizenship, Thind was from northern India and, according to the race science, was Aryan, a category that race scientists associated with Caucasians. Aryans were mythologized by Europeans as a superior Indo-European race that existed in the ancient world. This racial designation is still known to us largely because the Nazi party and other groups invested in projects of White racial superiority co-opted it as their own.

The Supreme Court weighed Thind's scientific claim to Whiteness against their own perceptions of him. As a brown-skinned man who wore a turban and did not practice Christianity, Thind did not read as White, based on the court's vague preconceptions of Whiteness. The courts decided that the racial sciences did not provide accurate categorization for Thind, dismissing his lawyer's scientific argument that because he was a high-caste Hindu, he was pure-blooded Aryan. Whether the justices saw through the ruse (Thind was Sikh, not Hindu) or not, the courts decided that his caste and his brown skin made him unable to assimilate to Whiteness, thus nullifying any presumed genetic proximity to Whiteness.[5]

The Thind and Ozawa cases demonstrate that the US Supreme Court was quite comfortable shifting between epistemological frameworks, especially if it allowed them to make different judgments that had exactly the same implications. Thind was not granted citizenship because he was found to be unable to assimilate into the dominant White culture of the United States. He applied twice more for citizenship and was successful at last only because of a law that granted citizenship to all veterans of World War I, which Thind had fought in as a member of the US military. After these cases, the term *Caucasian* appeared in numerous others as a legal and biological category that cemented its legitimate meaning as the indicator of White racial identity.

The legal and scientific arguments used to deny Ozawa and Thind citizenship were in large part a response to fears of race mixing—of losing the obvious definitions of racial classification that allowed for identifying superior and inferior races. The "science" of eugenics followed, claiming to provide hard evidence of the identifiable differences between groups and ranking them according to a scale of heritable traits in order to control the genetic distribution of the US population. But even before this pseudo-science was used as a tool of mass extermination, its impact on the formation of racial identities, especially the categories of Black and White, was formidable. Without the system of slavery, the social barrier between Blacks and Whites no longer existed. In the 1870s, Jim Crow laws would legalize racial segregation under the same premise that allowed slavery:

God created the races to remain separate. One way to reinforce this ideology was the practice of racial terror lynchings, rooted, more often than not, in accusations against Black men for raping White women and based on a set of stereotypes that offer insight into the racialized meanings of sexual purity.

While laws against interracial marriage existed since the seventeenth century, after Emancipation and Reconstruction, their use and enforcement grew. Unlike segregation and lynching, most Blacks had few inclinations to refute or fear anti-miscegenation laws, so their enforcement had limited opposition. In the early twentieth century, purity movements within Black communities emphasized "racial betterment" as a stepping stone toward middle-class status. Prioritizing the well-being of African American communities sometimes included a belief in racial purity, but primarily for the sake of security and self-sufficiency, not racial dominance. Even during the Civil Rights Movement of the 1960s, no legislation was ever considered or proposed to challenge the constitutionality of anti-miscegenation law. It took a modest interracial couple with the last name of Loving, who simply wanted to live their life together with their children and extended family, to end it all.

In 1958, Richard and Mildred Loving were legally married in Washington, DC, but lived in Virginia, where their marriage was not legally recognized. Just five weeks after their wedding, they were arrested at their home in the middle of the night. The judge found them guilty of breaking Virginia law and required them to live in DC, away from their extended family. When the American Civil Liberties Union (ACLU) took their case, it felt confident of a win, as the judge in Virginia had made use of a religious myth to uphold the law.[6] Once again, the story of Noah and his sons was deployed (in a courtroom no less) to validate a law enforcing racial separation. Though forthcoming civil rights legislation from the federal government did not include the right to marry across racial lines, the ACLU was able to overturn the ruling against the Lovings and ultimately get the Supreme Court to declare all anti-miscegenation laws unconstitutional.

Today we speak about White racial identity with wildly varying degrees of understanding and discomfort. Conservative politicians and other pundits use the concept to argue that White people are discriminated against because of their race. But what they are responding to are systemic critiques of Whiteness as a system of racial domination that has shaped every social institution we engage with. White racial dominance is not only dangerous because believing White people are better is a problematic assertion. It's dangerous because it anoints White people with the right to racial ignorance, encouraging us to reinforce the status quo and to explain inequality and the hardship of other racial groups as self-inflicted.

For scholars of race, contemporary Whiteness is a set of habits rooted in an imagined past that has been exonerated from injustice. Whiteness preserves this innocence with the same ferocity that it protected the presumed innocence of White women from Black male rapists. In both instances, a set cognitive habits shaped by denial, ignorance, and self-preservation create a White imaginary or racial imagination that is always working to normalize racial inequality.

For White evangelicals, the family serves as a useful tool for cultivating the White racial imagination. Defending the family as a hetero-patriarchal institution is indistinguishable from a defense of the faith. It offers a clear-cut moral trajectory for the nation to maintain the belief that it has a special relationship with God, one that is maintained, as so many White evangelicals believe, through the restrictive scripting of gender and sexuality. In her book *The Divine Institution: White Evangelicalism's Politics of the Family*, anthropologist Sophie Bjork-James astutely frames this as a White evasion tactic—a way to shift national debates away from White supremacy and racism, while also functioning to maintain the racial caste system.[7] White evangelicals remain stuck in a definition of racism that emphasizes individual sin, rather than structural injustice. Furthermore, the social importance given to the White family institution reinforces misunderstandings of how White supremacy functions. As Bjork-James explains, for White evangelicals all social problems are a result of families composed of individuals who are unable to embody God-anointed gender and sexual identities. Working toward obedience to what they see as God-given sexual and gendered identities, White evangelicals maintain that proper ordering of the family is the foundation for a properly ordered society. In this formulation, White evangelicals fail to consider their families as participating in a racial landscape, thus framing all social ills around sex and gender, the construction of the problem demonstrates the menacing nature of color-evasive racism. This is why many faith communities of color do not identify with the family-first politics of Christian nationalism, as they have long been aware that gender/sexual conservatism is a tool White Americans deploy in order to maintain racial superiority and racial segregation.[8]

In his book *The Myth of Color-Blind Christians: Evangelicals and White Supremacy in the Civil Rights Era*, historian Jesse Curtis examines how White evangelicals responded to the national call for racial equality by prioritizing racial reconciliation and color-evasive theology over racial justice.[9] Together, these strategies not only inhibit the task of racial equity but also allow White evangelicals to maintain racial virtue and moral authority. Color-evasive racism and projects on racial reconciliation prioritize the good intentions put toward addressing the problem of racism. However, an emphasis on racism as individual sin minimizes the work of racial justice by focusing on the individual healing of racist habits and attitudes. In this formulation, anti-racist work becomes highly spiritualized—another way for White people to perform penance and believe themselves to have worked out their sin. As a result, anti-racism is coopted into a task for the moral redemption of White people, who avoid doing the hard work of acknowledging and changing organizations, institutions, and social norms that enforce systemic oppression. Though groups that use scripture to support racial superiority and segregation were pushed to the social margins by the late twentieth century, our racial caste system remains in place because of an inability to acknowledge and examine White racial identity as the embodiment of that system.

Sociologist Joe Feagin's book *The White Racial Frame: Centuries of Racial Framing and Counter-Framing*, explains how individual behaviors and attitudes are grounded in a unique epistemology of Whiteness.[10] Knowing what is real, true, and good is a human instinct, often legible as feelings before thoughts. In the White imagination, US history is a narrative of national and religious exceptionalism, with genocide, slavery, and other atrocities explained away as "in the past" or "a past that has been corrected." Though expanded historical inquiry and religious literacy have shifted this in recent decades, backlash against this progress has resurfaced along social and political fault lines.

According to Feagin, Whiteness maintains virtue through its commitment to color evasion, the belief and practice that ignoring racial difference will ease racial discomfort (which it does for White people) and racial discrimination experienced by people of color (which it does not).[11] Color-evasive ideology makes several claims that reinforce the myth of White virtue: (1) racism is a set of personal behaviors and attitudes, not an embedded set of social norms and institutions that create structural inequality; (2) acknowledging racial inequality is a political tool used to promote left-leaning political ideologies; (3) learning the history of racism and other forms of inequality in the United States reinforces inequality by creating a "grievance class" that is given the moral and political upper hand; and (4) focusing less on racial identity creates a better outcome for achieving racial equality.

Having taught courses on the history of racism and religious discrimination for over a decade, I have an adequate grasp of what information students bring to my classroom. I have also watched how the work of Black Lives Matter and especially the racial reckoning during the summer of George Floyd's murder have impacted my students' ability to engage in these difficult conversations and to acknowledge the degree to which they have been miseducated about racial inequality. Most learn that slavery was bad but that "we" ended it. They learn that Dr. Martin Luther King Jr. led a peaceful protest movement that was successful because it was free of violence and rooted in Christianity. King's legacy is held up as preferable when compared to Malcolm X's "by any means necessary" approach. When I was a high school student, I came to the conclusion that Malcolm X was a Black Panther, my White imagination conflating all angry Black men and reducing their political and social critiques to unrighteous anger. While Malcolm's autobiography was highly regarded by the Black Panthers, he had been dead for several years before the organization ever emerged. I tell my students this every semester, after I've asked them if they too learned that Malcolm X was a Black Panther. (A few always have.)

Studying history, I assert, is one way to debunk the assumptions of our White racial imaginations. Overwhelmingly, my students have never spent significant time studying Native American or African American history. Though there are exceptions, my students themselves often agree that much of the history we cover was never explored in their pre-college education. This is a good example of how White racial habits form collective practices. Debates over how we teach history, are debates over history itself and, ultimately, about what the United States is as a nation. Historical truth telling and clear-eyed investigation are not inaccessible, but they rely on White people being willing to see and tell the truth. White racial identity, unfortunately, has been constructed to do just the opposite. The White racial frame is constructed to protect White people from having to tell and sit with the truth; it inoculates us against racial discomfort, perpetuating what sociologist Jennifer Mueller calls White racial ignorance.

Mueller describes White racial ignorance as a way that people rationalize *not* learning to or seeking to understand racial discrimination from information that is readily available. Non-knowledge is cultivated with intentionality, by individuals and institutions, in order to maintain the status quo, regardless of its promotion of systemic inequality.[12] In the next two chapters, we'll see the ways that White racial ignorance intersects with evangelical purity culture, itself an apt example of non-knowledge: young people are discouraged from learning about their bodies and its desires in order to promote sexual ignorance with the assumption that a lack of sexual understanding will prevent sexual activity. As an innocence myth, purity culture sits at the nexus of White racial and sexual ignorance.

CHAPTER FIVE

SEXUAL PURITY AND RACIAL FORMATIONS

S OCIAL MOVEMENTS AND IDENTITIES are informed by collective acts of resistance to oppressive systems but also in acquiescence to those same systems. As the history of feminism demonstrates, White women often elect officials to support the White status quo, even choosing to vote against their best interest. This is because the White status quo is a system of power that benefits White women, if we are willing to limit our own agency. While White women's achievements can appear to be a forward movement toward gender and sexual liberation, White women's power often comes from our proximity to White men's power and from White women learning to replicate the same patriarchal systems that deny other women and people of color access to resources and opportunities that facilitate human flourishing. The concept of *White feminism*, used to identity a failure of feminist politics, points toward upward mobility for White women at the expense of people of color, a phenomenon that has replayed itself over and over in the history of the United States.

Evangelical purity culture is a contemporary iteration of a particular set of racialized gender norms that first became salient in the nineteenth century. As a socially constructed category, White womanhood has a particular history that functions independently of White women's actual lived experiences, yet it exists to offer White women a set of privileges, opportunities, and securities that reaffirm the social order of a White, Christian nation. In short, White women who ally themselves with patriarchal power claim an entitlement to security and stability that they assert on behalf of their own families. The current fixation on "parental rights" used by parents who are anti-trans and anti–critical race theory at your local school board meeting is an extension of this set of privileges. Organizations such as Moms for Liberty fight for the right to protect one's children from a carefully cultivated set of fears, not from mass shootings or a global pandemic but from sexual, racial, and other forms of diversity that could make a White child (or a White parent) express emotional discomfort or cognitive dissonance.

Part of our contemporary debate around race derives from the lasting impact of slavery—on the lives of the descendants of enslaved people and on the nation as a whole. Though Christian concern about sexual purity began long before the history of Protestantism in the United States, the unique role of sexually pure White womanhood within US nation building offers a starting point in our efforts to understand the ways that sexual purity functions within a White supremacist framework. Because the institution of slavery created a sharp racial line between Black and White, those racial identities formed in contradistinction to one another. This was practical for those who sought to maintain slavery as an economic and social order. Within it, White women and Black women had vastly different experiences, especially in regard to sexuality and childbearing. Sexual purity was understood to be a female virtue that valorized White womanhood and the moral authority that came with childbearing, supporting an idealized family unit, even if women's and girl's experiences within those families were less than ideal. Enslaved Black women did not benefit from idealized family structures, nor did they have any control over their own bodies or the fate of the children they birthed. In the North, abolitionists understood the unique dilemma that enslaved Black women faced and used these stories of corrupted virtue to highlight the cruelty of the system.

In 1861, Harriet Jacobs published a memoir depicting her experiences being raised in, surviving, and eventually escaping slavery. She was invited by a circle of White women abolitionists to prepare her story for publication in hopes of growing the opposition toward slavery among Northerners. Though Jacobs was literate, she wrote alongside a White woman, Lydia Marie Child, to craft her story, which detailed the sexual danger she endured as an enslaved woman. Jacobs's story was carefully rendered to appeal to a genteel audience, highlighting her unique experiences as a woman. This meant going public with events and choices that most respectable people at the time would have found alarming. But that was the point—to raise the alarm about slavery, in part, by detailing the sexual degradation of women, a portrait that sharply contrasted with Christian virtues associated with femininity and motherhood.

As the formal property of the young daughter of a slave-owning family, Jacobs spent much of her young life in the household of the man she refers to as Dr. Flint. By the time she was an adolescent, Jacobs was already aware of Flint's desire to use her for his own sexual exploits. It was common for slave owners to groom young women for a sexual relationship, providing them with gifts and attention from a young age. Describing a life of severely limited sexual and physical autonomy, Jacobs treaded carefully for her more delicate readers and protected her own identity by using the pen name Linda Brent. She did not hold back but also implored her readers to understand why she could not prioritize her own sexual purity.

But, O, ye happy women, whose purity has been sheltered from childhood, who have been free to choose the objects of your affection, whose homes are protected by law, do not judge the poor desolate slave girl too severely! If slavery had been abolished, I, also, could have married the man of my choice; I could have had a home shielded by the laws; and I should have been spared the painful task of confessing what I am now about to relate; but all my prospects had been blighted by slavery.[1]

Jacobs's description of sexual purity indicates that the conditions of slavery were incommensurate with living a virtuous life, allowing Jacobs and her readers together to affirm the value of purity as a condition of a good life. A pure life is a protected life, in which laws and morals serve to enhance the lives of women, not degrade them. A pure life is also a life of freedom, in which women are able to choose whom they marry. Jacobs, of course, had neither. Instead, her story describes a young, desperate but bold teenager fearful of an increasingly sinister and predatory slave owner. She already lived outside the legal and moral systems of sexual purity, which could possibly merit protection and freedom. As such, it was outside those same systems where she found protection and eventually freedom.

In her autobiography, Jacobs confesses to beginning an illicit relationship with another White man, knowing that honor between White men would keep Flint away from her. Mr. Sands, as she called him, was at least kind and caring and came with promises of freedom and protection, though it meant sacrificing her virtue to gain these. When her grandmother learns of Harriet's first pregnancy, she assumes Flint has won her over. In disgust, she remarked,

"O Linda! has it come to this? I had rather see you dead than to see you as you now are. You are a disgrace to your dead mother." She tore from my fingers my mother's wedding ring and her silver thimble. "Go away!" she exclaimed, "and never come to my house, again." Her reproaches fell so hot and heavy, that they left me no chance to answer.[2]

The rift between Jacobs and her grandmother wouldn't last long, though the pain Jacobs endured was significant. Both understood that, within slavery, sexual abstinence was the one rare opportunity to maintain bodily autonomy. But without freedom, Jacobs had no means of protection within the legal structures that shaped her life.

It's notable that sexual purity is the one topic Jacobs chooses to address with her readers directly, likely hoping that the scene of reconciliation with her grandmother would earn the same sentiment from her readers. Though Jacobs was subject to unfathomable injustice, she had to present herself as complicit in her own self-ruin. She reminds readers regularly that she made the deliberate choice to begin a relationship with Mr. Sands and to have his children without any promise of marriage.

Jacobs's goal in writing her story was to gain the sympathy of northern White women and alert them to the plight of enslaved women in the South. She boldly described the sexual threats she endured and the choices she was compelled to make. She even suggests that those choices kept her from living "as a Christian." Just speaking publicly about one's intimate life was an assault on the Christian morality that characterized the nineteenth century. By portraying herself as a decision-maker and accepting responsibility for breeching one of the cardinal virtues of femininity, she maintained her stated claim to truth-telling, even when it pushed her beyond the limits of respectability.

Incidents in the Life of a Slave Girl was written for an audience of White women in the North. Jacobs's use of the theme of sexual purity was strategic, as her audience was shaped by the White Protestant virtue of true womanhood. Jacobs's descriptions of sexual danger, and her decision to reject sexual purity in the hope of attaining safety and freedom, meant she would never be acknowledged as having the same moral authority as White, middle-class women.

The racialization of White womanhood coalesced in the late nineteenth and twentieth centuries around myths of innocence and civilized virtue. Heavily promoted by first-wave feminism, representations of White womanhood fixated on women's symbolic and biological maternity. National virtues of justice, temperance, liberty, and progress were all embodied as White women, whose integrity guarded the threshold between civilization and barbarism, White and non-White, security and chaos. As such, White women's racial and sexual purity also symbolized the purported innocence of the US nation-state. This is shown in John Gast's *American Progress*, the commissioned painting used to illustrate a travel guide to Indian Country, more commonly known by White Americans as "the western frontier."

The painting depicts an ethereal female subject (my students sometimes identity her as an angel) who floats westward across the US landscape. She carries with her a schoolbook and telegraph wire, symbolizing the value of education and technology to the march of civilization. Before her is a darkened landscape that depicts wild animals and Indigenous people fleeing her arrival. Behind her, the landscape brightens, with a glimpse of a harbor where commerce is thriving. White men with domesticated animals follow behind her, prepared to claim the land for farming. The centrality of a White woman in Gast's work was no accident, as middle-class Protestants already understood that White women were granted a special status in the American experiment and represented the promise of an advancing American civilization.

White women exploited this special status in order to fight toward full political enfranchisement. In doing so, they participated in a set of racial stereotypes that distinguished them from non-White women, sexual purity being the most prominent. For Jacobs, sexual purity was about her sexual autonomy and the need to protect her future children. But for the White racist communities, sexual purity was a way to maintain racial separation and segregation.

After the emancipation of enslaved people, another set of stereotypes emerged: Black men who preyed upon White women. White racist communities relied on both of these stereotypes to assert the need to protect White women from the sexual violence of Black men.

Threats, or even rumors of threats, to White women's sexual purity became a pretext for White communities to punish Black people.

In 1892, Ida B. Wells began reporting on the practice of lynching in her newspaper the *Free Speech*, of Memphis, Tennessee. Three of her friends has been murdered by a mob after being accused of raping White women (though more likely they were targeted by rival shopkeepers). In her writing on lynching, she presented the events in stark detail, describing how the naked bodies of Black men were tortured and mutilated both before and after death. The men who became victims of lynching were often already incarcerated when White mobs broke into prisons to kidnap them and enact their own brutal form of vigilante justice. The purpose here wasn't merely to punish a crime but to demonstrate that White racial dominance remained intact even after the emancipation of enslaved people. Victims' bodies were riddled with bullets, branded, castrated, burned, and hanged. These were not clandestine acts committed to protect the identity of the perpetrators. These atrocities were committed in the light of day, often with large crowds gathering for a glimpse of the corpses on public display. It was a spectacle, a celebration of White power, with people clamoring for pieces of bone as souvenirs and purchasing postcards to commemorate the murder of a Black man.

Wells's work on anti-lynching campaigns provided a critical lens through which to view the sexual racism that terrorized Black people after the Civil War. Without the social and racial order of slavery, White Southerners sought to reinforce their racial power as soon as Reconstruction ended. Segregation of the races remained a social and theological mandate, with Whites implementing various forms of violence to maintain the race line.

Wells's investigation into racial terror lynchings exposed the set of racialized sexual stereotypes that also animated the nineteenth-century purity movement. She clarified for the nation that "the lynching myth," which justified mob violence against and the brutal murders of thousands of Black people between 1870 and 1950, was composed of two falsehoods: Black men were over-sexed rapists, and White women's innate sexual purity did not permit them to consent to sexual relationships with Black men. Wells's coverage of these stories included her complete dismissal of rape allegations:

> Nobody in this section of the country believes the old thread-bare lie that Negro men rape White women. If Southern white men are not careful, they will overreach themselves and public sentiment will have a reaction; a conclusion will then be reached which will be very damaging to the moral reputation of their women.[3]

It was evident to Wells that White women's purity was an ideological wedge used to pathologize miscegenation and to maintain the race line between Black and White. Out of town at the time, reaction to Wells's words was swift. A violent mob burned her newspaper office, and their threats of physical violence made Wells a fugitive. She had exposed the falsehoods used in White communities to justify racial violence:

> The Southern white man says that it is impossible for a voluntary alliance to exist between a white woman and a colored man, and therefore, the fact of an alliance is a proof of force. In numerous instances where colored men have been lynched on the charge of rape, it was positively known at the time of lynching, and indisputably proven after the victim's death, that the relationship sustained between the man and woman was voluntary and clandestine, and that in no court of law could even the charge of assault have been successfully maintained.[4]

It was the recognition of relations between Black men and White women as "voluntary and clandestine" that shattered the illusion of White women's sexual purity.

It wasn't just White Southerners who refused to accept Wells's conclusions. Frances Willard was president of the Woman's Christian Temperance Union (WCTU), the most prominent women's organization of the late nineteenth century. Though its primary work focused on "home protection," namely, the ills associated with alcohol, and eventually women's suffrage, it also played a significant role in promoting "social purity" (a demure alternative to sexual purity) through direct outreach, including encouraging young people to take purity pledges. Like many White reformers, Willard asserted that White women's purity was a natural trait, one that situated her and her colleagues as moral arbiters granted the providential right to expand their influence over US social and political life.

As she explained in her 1890 speech "A White Life for Two":

> With all my heart I believe, as do the best men of the nation, that woman will bless and brighten every place she enters, and that she will enter every place on the round earth. Its welcome of her presence and her power will be the final test of any institution's fitness to survive.[5]

Willard believed that White women's power lay in their moral authority, a status that rested on the racialized stereotype of White women's sexual innocence. Purity ideology served the goal of creating a nation-state ruled by White Anglo-Saxon Protestants and as such provided White women a platform from which to secure greater political power. When Wells challenged the authenticity of White women's purity, she also threatened the political power that White women were striving for.

Also in 1890, Frances Willard gave an interview, published as "The Race Problem," in which she describes her concerns over race mixing. Despite biographical statements in which she situated herself and her family squarely in the abolitionist movement, Willard also asserted that all racial groups were stronger when "pure-blooded" and even said that were she of African descent she would long to return to Africa.

> I should go where my color was the correct thing, and leave these
> pale faces to work out their own destiny; and I should build in my
> life to make my color fashionable by as much as one individually
> could do it.[6]

Willard believed that race mixing signified civilizational decline, though it's unclear if her opposition to slavery was due in part to her opposition to race mixing. But now that the separation between Black and White was less possible due to emancipation, she appeared to be advocating that Blacks and Whites protect their own bloodlines in order to preserve the futures of their respective races.

The comment in this interview that most provoked readers, including Ida B. Wells, was Willard's sympathetic regard for White Southerners who navigated the purported threats posed to them by Blacks in the South.

> I pity the Southerners; and I believe the great mass of them are as
> conscientious, and kindly-intentioned toward the colored man, as
> an equal number of white church members at the North. Would-
> be demagogues lead the colored people to destruction. [. . .] The
> problem on their hands is immeasurable. The colored race multi-
> plies like the locusts of Egypt. The grog shop is the center of power.
> The safety of women, of childhood, of the home, is menaced in a
> thousand localities at this moment, so that men dare not go beyond
> the sight of their own roof-tree.[7]

The "locusts of Egypt" is a reference to the Exodus story, which was particularly meaningful to enslaved converts to Christianity, as it narrated a story of slaves freed from captivity. Willard's choice to use the Exodus story to describe freedmen and -women in a derogatory way is especially cruel. Her comments become even more troubling when you consider that by 1890 the practice of lynching had become a regular feature of Southern life.

Numerous historians agree with Wells's analysis that lynching emerged post-Emancipation as a practice of White terrorism against newly enfranchised African American men. With slavery dismantled, there was no formal way for Whites to maintain their superior status, and with the Thirteenth, Fourteenth, and Fifteenth Amendments to the Constitution providing Black women and men citizenship, and Black men the right to vote, Southern Whites sought to reinforce racial hierarchies in the cruelest way possible.

Frances Willard's and other purity activists' commitment to "social purity" functioned as a bulwark of first-wave feminism. When Willard expressed sympathy for Southern Whites, whom she believed were under siege by drunken, violent Black men, she provided an institutional sanction for both sexual stereotypes. It's not at all surprising to note that, at this time, Willard was working to increase Southern membership in the WCTU and so found numerous ways to deflect Wells's accusations of White women's complicity. Like White Southern men, Willard could neither imagine nor allow these relationships to be seen as consensual, as her political machine ran on the fuel of White women's moral authority, an authority easily undercut by revelations of a "voluntary alliance" between White women and Black men. At the WCTU's national meeting in 1894, Willard publicly rebuked Wells:

> It is my firm belief that in the statements made by Miss Wells concerning white women having taken the initiative in nameless acts between the races she has put an imputation upon half the white race in this country that is unjust, and, save in the rarest exceptional instances, wholly without foundation.[8]

This is what Willard knew: White women's purity was not ultimately about personal morality but about maintaining a social order.
By advocating purity in this way, Willard worked to maintain the
color line, which meant making every effort to discredit Wells. This
is especially curious, because Wells herself never attacked the ideal
of purity as a form of personal morality. Wells's writings were deeply
infused with the honorifics of social purity, even as she challenged the
veracity of White women's claims. The virtue of honesty, for Wells, far
surpassed any need to protect a culture of purity that required silence
around sexuality. This comes into clear relief in her public debates
with Willard, who took great umbrage at Wells's truth-telling about
"Black Sampsons and White Delilahs."[9]

Wells's revelations were specific to the crimes she investigated.
She was calling out the White women who stood by while their
lovers were imprisoned and brutalized by White mobs, though she
also noted that White communities would use violence and threats
of violence to pressure White women to report their Black lovers.
In one case, a woman in this situation was also required to light the
matched that burned her lover to death. As she did so, the victim
declared, "Why are you doing this when we've been sweet-hearting
for so long."[10] The weight of a White woman's reputation rested heavily on the community, functioning as the boundary marker between
White and Black, between purity and impurity. When that boundary
was threatened, reaction was fierce and violent, the social pressures
coercing a once amorous partner to turn on her beloved.

Other African American moral reformers also understood that
social purity was a strategic tool for racial uplift and a way to resist
sexual racism if it could be uncoupled from White racial identity.
Activists such as Frances Ellen Watkins Harper, Lucy Thurman,
and Fannie Barrier Williams advocated for social purity in their
work alongside White reformers and within their own communities.
Harper, a member of the WCTU, was the only person of color to
speak at the National Purity Congress in 1895. She spoke of a rescue

organization that would not help a Black prostitute who came to it for assistance: "As crime has neither sex nor color, so its prevention and remedies should not be hampered by either race or sex limitations."[11] Harper's comment, like Wells's before her, sought to decouple purity and criminality from certain racialized contexts.

Frances Ellen Watkins Harper openly condemned lynching, even as she called for increased attention to purity work among her people, not because they required "sympathy and charity" but because they were full citizens entitled to the same protections under the US Constitution. She and Lucy Thurman expanded the initiatives of the Woman's Christian Temperance Union by creating the Department of Work Among the Colored People, which focused on promoting purity in Black communities.

At the 1893 Parliament of the World's Religions, Fannie Barrier Williams challenged the purity movement by calling into question White women's exclusive claim to moral authority—a position, she argued, that was obtained at the expense of Black women. White women's moral authority implied the moral inferiority of Black women. Domestic femininity, not racial identity, Williams argued, was the key to social and moral uplift.

> We do not yet sufficiently appreciate the fact that the heart of every social evil and disorder among the colored people, especially of the rural South, is the lack of those inherent moral potencies of home and family that are the well-springs of all the good in human society.[12]

Because our current historiography of sexual purity is framed within debates over gender and sexuality alone, it does not adequately attend to the contributions of these women. Wells, Williams, Harper, and Thurman challenged the seemingly providential ties between White women's sexual innocence and White racial superiority. In doing so they revealed that purity ideologies were profoundly influenced by debates over racial identity and inequality. Their work decoupled purity from Whiteness, contested the racist imagination of White America, and established a collective commitment to sexual purity for the purposes of elevating their entire race to middle-class respectability.

Despite these claims by Black women, some of whom were in her own organization, the WCTU, Frances Willard clung to her belief that White women held the primary, if not the exclusive, right to the benefits of sexual purity. Like many White reformers, Willard believed that White women's purity and moral authority were threatened by mere rumors of miscegenation. While White purity reformers did not produce the science or legislation that formally instituted racial separation, purity ideologies provided the religious and moral argument for racial separation by linking White women's virtue to the moral status of the nation-state.

The racial formation of White womanhood writ large is rooted in long-standing nationalistic tropes embedded in the White imagination because of fears of racial mixing and violence against White women. While these represent the actual fears of powerful White people in the late nineteenth and early twentieth centuries, the meanings of White womanhood hold a cultural power far beyond the historic contexts in which it is most salient. To say that White womanhood continues to inform the White racial imagination with an extensive catalogue of meanings and protective measures is not an overstatement. Establishing White womanhood as quintessentially American, as embodying the promise of economic and social flourishing has grown into a set of gendered habits, actions, and beliefs that continue to grant White women moral authority.

CHAPTER SIX

SEXUAL PURITY AND RACIAL DISEMBODIMENT

A IMEE WAS BORN in and raised outside Atlanta, Georgia. She was one of the few White participants in the After Purity Project who spoke openly about her racial identity. At a young age she was aware that she lived in a racially integrated world but one that was highly stratified. As children growing up in the South, she and her White friends had developed physically intimate relationships with the Black women who worked as their caregivers. In fact, when Aimee did have a nanny who was White, many of her friends marveled at the anomaly. She observed the deferential treatment her family received at their country club, where all the members shared their race but where the staff were entirely Black. When she asked her parents about this, she was ordered to hush and was told: "That's just how things are. They get paid very well. And they are happy to do this job.¹"

Not only had Aimee had been taught not to question the racial status quo around her; she also had been taught it was improper to even speak about race. The conservative Methodist Church she attended had been used during the Civil War as a Confederate hospital, the names of soldiers carved into outdoor benches. It was a church with an all-White membership; the only Black people worked to provide nursery care during services. Until high school, Aimee attended what historians now call a "segregation academy," one of many private Christian schools founded after school desegregation that allowed White Christians to continue sending their children to all-White schools. In high school, images of the Confederate flag were ubiquitous on cars driven by her classmates, a symbol of White Southern pride and heritage.

Though well-traveled throughout Europe, Aimee arrived at college in the northeastern United States never having traveled north of South Carolina. One of her most treasured possessions was a pillow, handmade by her best friend, made from the Georgia state flag, which at the time included the Confederate stars and bars.[2] When her roommate, a person of color, confronted her, using words like "wrong, offensive, and racist," Aimee could not comprehend her anger. When the roommate demanded that Aimee remove or destroy the pillow, Aimee responded with anger and defensiveness. *How could the entire state of Georgia be racist?*, she thought. Aimee was experiencing what psychologists call *cognitive dissonance*, when a piece of information completely upends a previously accepted reality. It can unmoor people's sense of identity, community, and stability, often arousing strong feelings.

In our interview, Aimee recalled feeling shame and embarrassment about what she didn't know and about how unprepared she was to address the White supremacy that had shaped her. Aimee was an academically gifted student who took pride in gathering knowledge. In our interview, I perceived that her shame at age seventeen was wrapped up in a growing awareness that she had been severely miseducated. She was concerned with holding herself accountable for not taking her AP history courses seriously. She felt ashamed that it took a confrontation with a person of color, with whom she was trying to build a good relationship, for her to become aware of the deficit. So Aimee did the work. She studied and learned the history of the Confederate flag and came to understand why it provoked strong reactions. She was able to apologize to her roommate and gained enough confidence to continue investigating her own racial identity.

Aimee used the word *culpability* in our interview several times. She is highly educated and has spent a great deal of time thinking about how she holds responsibility for the racist past and present, a responsibility that demands her understanding of the nature and extent of White supremacy in the United States. She finds Jennifer Mueller's concept of White racial ignorance an apt descriptor of the color-evasive lessons she learned growing up.[3] Her story is not unique, nor particular to one raised in the South. Whiteness is a racial identity that fosters ignorance about itself, even claiming this ignorance is a virtue when it comes to addressing the problem of racism.

Tracing the history of sexual purity as a racialized concept helps us see the truth that so-called color-evasion attempts to conceal. Because White womanhood, as we saw in the previous chapter, came to represent both a sexual and racial ideal, and because it remains such an important symbol in the evangelical world today, we can now see that a particularly sexualized racism remains deeply embedded in evangelical purity culture. Both then and today, restraints on White women's sexual agency, or at least the appearance of such, serves as a symbol of White racial superiority. Those of us socialized into evangelical purity culture are formed by an unarticulated White racial ideal. If we are White, this means internalizing a sense of our own racial superiority and learning to see our racial power as a form of personal empowerment (sometimes even framed as a form of feminism) while remaining unaware of the racial dynamics we participate in.

For those who are not White, this formation process means absorbing racist stereotypes around sexuality and navigating a religious culture that demands practices of racial and sexual disembodiment. Shawna, one of the few women of color I interviewed for the After Purity Project, is a self-described military brat who was raised in the Southern Baptist Church. She identifies as Black/biracial and as an adult referred to herself as a "recovering Southern Baptist" until she realized others perceived it as disrespectful rather than part of her process of spiritual questioning. Though Shawna acknowledges she is still in the process of recovery, she prefers to describe herself as ex-vangelical.

Shawna views purity culture as a deeply "unhealthy system" that asks young people to control a natural set of instincts, which she learned to regard as "evil." She recalls learning to question her relationships with men, whom she was told to see as dangerous due to their presumed sexual voraciousness. Shawna describes herself at this time as a "super-judgy" teenager who was concerned with establishing her Christian credibility. She always wanted to do the right thing in order to demonstrate that she was better than everybody. But behind her piety was a deep fear of going to hell, a fear that robbed her of any of the "joy and lightness" she saw in other Christians. She also resented feeling like she had to evangelize to non-Christians, which made her feel like a bad Christian.

Despite these misgivings, Shawna was all in. She became deeply involved in an intentional community and participated in short-term mission work, which allowed her to develop a more sophisticated understanding of missionary work, one focused on providing social services rather than soul-saving. She was getting more serious about serving as a full-time missionary when she started a relationship with an atheist, who helped her to realize that her beliefs no longer matched those of the Southern Baptist Church.

When I asked Shawna why she signed up to be interviewed, she explained it was because academic studies of purity culture prioritize the experiences of White women, ignoring the experiences of women of color and neglecting to provide an analysis of race. Having watched the 2015 documentary *Give Me Sex Jesus*, she was able to make connections between purity culture and racial segregation. She told me, "Oh my God, that makes so much sense. You have to control women in order for White women to maintain the purity of the White race."

More recent scholarship is starting to attend to the racial gap Shawna notes. In the article "Decolonizing Purity Culture: Gendered Racism and White Idealization in Evangelical Christianity," lead author Madison Natarajan and her collaborators note a lack of research focusing on the experiences of women of color in purity culture.[4] They argue that purity culture teachings that "perpetuate whiteness by situating the ideal embodiment of sexual purity in attractive white girls" center those experiences alone. Following suit, studies of purity culture further marginalize the experiences of women of color by focusing on the needs of White women, such as learning sexual autonomy and recovering from sexual trauma. But for women of color, Natarajan contends, purity-culture analysis requires the use of intersectionality and critical race feminism in order to address how gender, sex, and race function together within systems of privilege and oppression.

In October 2015, the newly married Brelyn Bowman presented her father with a gift: a certificate signed by her personal physician declaring that she was sexually pure. Brelyn and her husband, Tim Bowman Jr., proudly displayed on their personal social media accounts a photo, taken at the wedding reception, of the new Mrs. Bowman and her father holding the certificate. On the flight to their honeymoon in Dubai, the couple discovered the post had gone viral and garnered a significant amount of criticism, including calling the father and daughter's decision "wacko," "savage," and "gross." Undaunted by their detractors, the Bowmans spent the next three years promoting sexual purity, with Bre publishing the book *No Ring No Ting*, which details her self-initiated commitment to sexual purity at the age of thirteen until her marriage.[5]

The public reaction to the Bowmans' wedding photo was echoed by numerous media outlets, which sought out the Bowmans to discuss their premarital chastity. Though most viewed the Bowmans as distinctive in their premarital virginity, they are not the first African Americans to publicly assert their claim to sexual purity. That several prominent media outlets perceived the Bowmans to represent an anomaly belies certain racist assumptions about African American sexuality and ignores how discourses around race interacted with purity teachings in their earliest iteration.

Contemporary evangelical purity culture is a product of a color-evasive, White evangelicalism that ignores racial difference and over-emphasizes the promises of racial reconciliation. But as a component of women's racial formation, evangelical purity culture invests in a system of sexual racism that controls the degree to which women can access bodily autonomy. This does not mean that women of color have been uninterested in engaging with the purity ideal—just the opposite. In her forthcoming book, *Weaponizing Virtue: Black Women and Intimate Resistance in the Age of U.S. Expansion,* historian Kaisha Esty demonstrates that by adopting sexual purity, Black women, enslaved and free, were able to resist the sexual violence of White men. For enslaved women, protecting one's chastity was about personal virtue, yes, but also about protecting one's child-bearing. As Esty emphasized in my interview with her, protecting purity was less an individual task of maintaining respectability and more about holding community together in the present and the future.[6]

Likewise, Michelle Mitchell's *Righteous Propagation* examines how early twentieth-century Black communities adopted White purity ideologies to resist racist sexual stereotypes.[7] Sexual respectability was not simply about establishing middle-class manners, though that was a part. It was also about self-protection as racist sexual stereotypes about Black people justified waves of violence, including racial-terror lynchings and sexual assault. Mitchell goes on to describe how the embrace of purity allowed Black communities to practice "racial betterment," a set of projects that improved the quality of life of and established hope for the thriving of future generations of African Americans. In an historical moment when race scientists were labeling Black people as genetically inferior and predicting their extinction, the promotion of purity contributed to a thriving Black middle-class that held the promise of robust future generations.

The racial habits and stereotypes constructed vis-à-vis purity ideology in the late nineteenth and early twentieth centuries remain in play in today's evangelical purity culture. Looking at three differently racialized evangelical contexts, we can see how these stereotypes continue to inform the varying degrees of sexual and racial agency among Black, White, and Asian American women.

There is a robust disagreement among African American Christians about the virtue of sexual purity. Brelyn Bowman's story is only one point of engagement. Other women engaged with purity teachings—such as scholars Tamura Lomax, Monique Moultrie, and Brittney Cooper and writers Jasmine Holmes, Lyvonne Picou, Olivia Smarr, T. F. Charlton, and Keisha E. McKenzie—have publicly articulated and analyzed their experiences as fraught with racial and sexualized stereotypes, religious colonialism, misogynoir, and heterosexism. They make up a post-purity resistance among Black women whose work points to the long-standing connection between sexual purity and White racial dominance.

Fostered by the work of womanist and Black feminist theologians, numerous African American women have engaged in public conversations around the expectations and limitations of sexual purity as promoted in their predominantly Black churches. These conversations center on the unique experiences of Black women and engage the theological and historical questions that emerge at the intersections of religious identity, sanctioned sexual practices, and anti-Black racism. The dialectic between religion and sexuality for Black women seeking a sexual ethic outside evangelical purity culture addresses a desire for sexual wholeness and personal authenticity, regardless of how these women position themselves in relation to evangelical purity culture.

In 2011, Dr. Brittney Cooper broached the topic in her blog post "Single, Saved, and Sexin'," in which she made a bold confession: "I'm single. I'm saved (as in born-again Christian). And I have sex unapologetically."[8] The backlash from Christian readers was so fierce it took Cooper two years to address the topic again. She gathered a small group of clergy and scholars on YouTube that included Theresa Thames, Arabella Littlepage, and Candi Dugas to discuss how and why Black churches promote sexual conservatism, especially given how many embrace liberatory theological frameworks.[9]

Many of the criticisms the group raised demonstrate similarities between Black churches and White evangelical churches. The emphasis on sexual repression, the need to control female bodies, a deep discomfort about bodies and embodied practices, the infantilization of grown women who remain unmarried, and the sexual double-standard are features that White and Black evangelicalism have in common. Cooper noted that women in the church are taught to expect God to reward them with a husband if they demonstrate their faithfulness and remain chaste. But this elides significant sociological factors that have contributed to the growing number of Black women who are unable to find a partner. She went on to challenge the heterosexist assumptions that exist in many Christian churches by articulating that her search for a husband was simply not a priority. But she wasn't willing to put sex on hold out of obligation to church teachings that were not invested in her personal well-being.

In her book *Eloquent Rage: A Black Feminist Discovers Her Superpower*, Cooper reflects on her experiences growing up in White purity culture.[10] Raised in the Southern Baptist Church, Cooper had internalized the belief that sex was sinful, dangerous, and unhealthy, so she learned to avoid it as part of her strategy for achieving academic success and avoiding social shame. She was a Black teenager in a predominantly White school system, where she noticed that successful White students did not have sex and get pregnant. Before understanding how White privilege conceals the truth about racial disparities, Cooper came to associate purity with being a Christian and a good student—the kind who would not get caught with an unplanned pregnancy.

It was her grandmother that set Cooper straight at the age of twenty-two, encouraging her to consider that good sex is a responsibility to oneself, whether one is inside or outside the church. Cooper wrote that, in retrospect, she realized that by embracing purity teachings she had acquiesced to beliefs in White racial superiority.

> Many Black Christian girls are seduced by white evangelicalism, because, hell, it seems to be working out so well for white people. I mean, white Jesus helps white people to win a lot. But when my grandmother showed me that I could take a different approach to my theology, that it could be a push and pull, a debate, and even an ongoing set of arguments with God, she freed me up from my investment in being a Christian Goody Two-shoes.[11]

Cooper's analysis as a Black feminist scholar within the church helps us understand more deeply how evangelical purity culture promotes White racial dominance. Even as she and her colleagues criticize sexual conservatism within Black churches, they also recognize that these are sites where the power of White supremacy is mitigated by theologies of resistance and liberation. None of the women in Cooper's roundtable advocated leaving their churches or the Christian faith. Cooper even introduces the possibility that worship practices in Black churches are erotic experiences, as it is one place where "Black folks can show out with their body."[12]

Purity teachings in Black churches are distinct from those in White evangelicalism because they are the result of contending with sexual racism. As demonstrated in previous chapters, the history of sexual purity and anti-Black racism is littered with sexual stereotypes about Black women and men that remain pervasive within the White imagination. In their roundtable discussion with Cooper, Arabella Littlepage notes that Black people have always been expected to confirm to White racial and sexual norms. This has created a culture of sexual surveillance in Black churches, which understand that, under the White gaze, the missteps of one Black person reflect on the entire group.[13]

In the early twentieth century, Black churchwomen created a set of social norms drawn from White purity movements in order to keep community members aligned with respectable behavioral practices. In her study of these women, scholar Evelyn Brooks Higginbotham named this effort "the politics of respectability.[14]" According to womanist ethicist Monique Moultrie, an expert on purity teachings within Black churches, respectability politics at this time were meant to counter segregationist practices, which heightened fears of racial contamination.[15] Echoing Michelle Mitchell's argument about Black communities encouraging purity in order to defy racist stereotypes, the politics of respectability were a self-defensive measure: displaying the norms of respectability allowed Black people to counter anti-Black stereotypes of hypersexuality. Displays of sexual restraint were encouraged among Black churchwomen and -men so as not to evoke the suspicions of the White people they encountered.

The sexual racism that purity culture lodges against Black women is rife with assumptions about Black female bodies and the need to control them. Writer and educator Jasmine Holmes, who has blogged about growing up Black in the purity movement, learned that before marriage her modesty protected men whom she could possibly "cause to stumble" and that within marriage her body was a weapon used to keep her husband from straying."[16] As an adult trying to make sense of these teachings, Holmes determined that this sexual ethic reduces women and their bodies to a singular purpose: influencing the behaviors of men. As in many formulations of purity teachings, the task of maintaining male sexual purity, both marital and nonmarital falls to women.

Pastor Lyvonne Picou, whose work focuses on helping women of color heal from sexual trauma and shame, articulates the theological missteps of purity culture. Church communities, she argues, socialize women into the notion that their bodies and human sexuality are sinful and out of control. These teachings are not concerned with the flourishing of Black women; rather, they are in service to various systems of power. Though Picou does not further characterize these systems, another pastor, Keisha McKenzie, offers that purity teachings are a form of "religious colonialism" imported by White American evangelicals into communities of color in the US and abroad.[17]

In 2017, Black feminist religion scholar Tamura Lomax curated a set of essays entitled #BlackSkinWhiteSin, analyzing the work and impact of Juanita Bynum, a minister in the Church of God in Christ, whose message "No More Sheets" encourages women to embrace sexual conservatism.[18] Bynum's teachings are similar to those found in White purity culture, but as Lomax notes, the ideals of womanhood and the protections ascribed to them have never been fully available to Black women. Several authors in #BlackSkinWhiteSin describe Bynum's emphasis on holiness, as is characteristic of Pentecostal traditions. For Black women, Bynum defines holiness according to standards of physical and behavioral modesty, creating a stark dichotomy between spirit and flesh. While Lomax recognizes that these mandates are rooted in a desire to project respectability, she also points to the ways that Bynum is borrowing the logic of White supremacy to create her good/bad binary.[19]

In response to Bynum, whose teachings are just one example of how purity culture exists within Black religious spaces, Lomax brought together a group of Black feminist and womanist clergy and scholars to examine the impact of Bynum's ministry. Their aim was to refute myths and stereotypes that mark Black women as innately sexually deviant and to interrogate the assumption that sex and holiness are incompatible.

Monique Moultrie studied Bynum and the women who participate in her ministry in her first book, *Pious and Passionate: Religious Media and Black Women's Sexuality*.[20] Bynum, she explains, makes use of her own struggles to remain pure in order to connect with her audiences: instead of deploying unattainable ideals, she provides assurance to women who share her struggles. At the same time, Bynum teaches that actively embracing a sexually pure lifestyle is how women demonstrate their worthiness to enter into a partnership with a man. As Moultrie explains, "God grants husbands to women who have purified themselves."

Bynum's audience seeks her out because they share her belief that heterosexual marriage is necessary for a successful and joyful life, one that helps people enter into middle-class respectability and live a set of ideals that were created to designate White women as racially superior to other women. Bynum offers a solution for Black women controlled by the sexual stereotypes created by Whites to justify their belief in Black inferiority: live according to the set of exacting standards that demonstrate you are worthy; your body is under control, and your soul is saved.

In many ways, Bynum's teachings are a replication of purity teachings within White evangelicalism. Marriage is given salvific significance—it is a state of grace women must earn through sexual restraint and modest comportment. Heterosexuality is mandatory—acting upon same-sex attraction is sinful, rather than part of the spectrum of human sexuality. But Bynum's audience is different from the usual purity culture audience because they are grown women, not adolescents, seeking encouragement to remain celibate in preparation for marriage in an immediate future. These are also women who have experienced anti-Black racism around their sexuality. Celibacy is not just a practice of obedience but an act of resistance against racist and sexual stereotypes that continue to impact how Black women in particular meet, date, marry, and otherwise partner.

In her essay for the #BlackSkinWhiteSin series, Moultrie describes how Bynum understands the concept of holiness in relationship to sexuality.[21] In concert with her denomination, the Church of God in Christ (COGIC), Bynum teaches women that modesty in dress and adornment indicates one's submission to God and openness to the work of the Holy Spirit in one's life. Though Moultrie is one of many Black scholars who offer a critique of Bynum's work, she also reminds her reader that Black women seeking to reconcile their sexuality and their theology have few resources for doing so. Bynum offers a clear path with support and community, but, as Moultrie points out, it is a path that requires Black women to reinvest in patriarchal and White supremacist notions that expect performances of holiness that negate the body's need for attention and care. The practice of disembodiment as a signifier of holiness calms the White imagination, but it robs women of a significant life source. Moultrie calls upon her colleagues to develop alternatives that encourage Black women to navigate their sexuality and theological commitments in the contexts of their own embodied experiences.

The history of anti-Asian racism in the United States is easily whitewashed by the racial stereotype of the model minority, which portrays Asian immigrants as compliant and eager to assimilate to White Christian America. As a result, anti-Asian discrimination and violence often remains under the radar, except, of course, for those who experience it directly. For Asian Americans, being raised in evangelical purity culture has meant remaining mostly invisible in the public discourse around it. According to MiHee Kim-Cort, a pastor and doctoral student in US religious history, the processes of colonialism, immigration, and White supremacy have rendered "the Asian woman who is American . . . simultaneously translucent, a mirror and a looking glass; she is a ghost invisible, unknowable, stripped of her identity, making her both desirable and expendable."[22]

Anti-Asian fears are rooted in colonial, missionary, and military histories and national expansion projects in which Asian women were expected to be both hypersexualized and sexually compliant. American missionaries, Kim-Cort argues, concerned about the treatment of Asian women in these contexts, reinforced these stereotypes, which then became commonplace in the United States. For author Angie Hong, this means that Asian bodies, like African bodies, are perceived not as pure but as an "other" who is expected to conform to the ways of or serve as a foil to the good Christian woman.[23]

The myth of the model minority exists because of intense pressures placed upon Asian Americans to assimilate so they are perceived as nonthreatening to Whites. With the outbreak of COVID-19, anti-Asian bias and violence quickly surfaced, indicating that, despite all assimilation efforts, people of Asian descent are still perceived as a racialized, foreign threat in the US. As such, Hong continues, the benefits of upholding sexual purity are not available to Asian and Asian American women unless they are willing to support the ideologies of White supremacy, which demand the erasure of their identity.[24]

Kim-Cort and Hong are two of the many Asian Americans who helped us understand the massacre of six Asian American women at the hand of a young White man raised in the Southern Baptist Church. As discussed in chapter 2, Robert Aaron Long was twenty-one when he traveled to three different spas in the Atlanta area, shooting and killing women he believed were responsible for his struggle with sexual temptation. He was taught by his church that "adultery, fornication, homosexuality, bisexual conduct, bestiality, incest, polygamy, pedophilia, pornography, or any attempt to change one's sex, or disagreement with one's biological sex" is "sinful and offensive to God."[25] Shaped by the doctrines of purity culture, Long internalized a fear of his own sexuality and the objects of his desire, which he came to view as a sex addiction.

Though sex addiction is not included in the *Diagnostic and Statistical Manual of Mental Disorders*, evangelical Christian men, more so than any other group, speak about struggling with sexual desire as a disorder.[26] According to Hong, the language of sex addiction is one of the many ways that purity culture positions women as the cause of violence perpetuated by men. In the case of Long, Asian American women who worked at massage parlors were the cause of his problem. By eliminating them, he believed he could eliminate the problem of sexual temptation. Long's logic may have been warped by a mental health crisis, but his beliefs about sex and sin were entirely consistent with the teachings of sexual purity as promoted by his church.

While law enforcement and many journalists ignored the racist element in Long's motivations, Asian American women wrote extensively about long-established perceptions of Asian women as a sexual fetish. Kim-Cort notes how "the figure of the Asian woman in Asia and in diaspora, particularly the U.S., acts as a canvas on which expectations and anxieties around domesticity, sexuality, and nation-state converge to produce more than a scapegoat, but a particular objecthood and aesthetic that evokes a racialized femininity."[27] Whereas Black women are a foil to White womanhood, Asian American women are a blank canvas that can be painted to affirm or oppose White racial ideals of femininity.

In her article "The Flaw at the Center of Purity Culture" for *The Atlantic*, Angie Hong writes about how she internalized purity teachings as an adult working in a White evangelical church.[28] This included blaming herself for unwanted attention from male colleagues in ministry work. She diagnosed her shame as having been caused by her own guilt for making herself too alluring to the men she worked with. But once she understood that their behavior was rooted in a sexual stereotype, she unlocked one of the ways that purity culture had distorted her sense of self.

Both Kim-Cort and Hong agree that purity culture within Asian American contexts is about assimilation to White American Christian culture. Asian American churches that promote purity culture do so without raising questions about the colonial and missionary histories that created sexualized stereotypes. Instead, these churches use the teachings to reinforce authoritarian leadership styles that parallel those found in White evangelical churches.

While many religious communities struggle to understand why sexual violence happens within their circles, White evangelical communities are especially good at characterizing the problem as one that is not part of their community or theology. Aaron Long's church quickly unenrolled him from church membership. He had been baptized just three years prior and was a noted leader in his youth group, described by his former youth pastor as kind and dedicated to serving others. Long's actions required the church to cut all ties with him and condemn his behaviors as rooted, not in purity teachings or other theological claims of the church, but in his sin-filled heart.[29] The removal of Long and the condemnation of his actions by his church allowed the church to distance itself and its belief systems from Long's actions, and in doing so it failed to understand how purity ideology infected Long's sense of morality.

Much of the work of White evangelicalism in the United States is meant to maintain the appearance of respectability and virtue. I didn't understand this growing up in my small, parent-run Christian school, which I attended from kindergarten until high school graduation. Nor did I realize that, unlike the public school, only White students attended my school. I enjoyed the illusion of safety and the support of a tight-knit community. There wasn't much I needed to question, nor was I encouraged to do so. In the second grade, when I met a new student, a missionary kid from Japan, I was fascinated. I peppered her with requests to say words in Japanese and reveled in their strangeness. My young mind couldn't make sense of her racial identity because I associated her with Japan, but she didn't look Japanese to me. But she also didn't look like me. (She was of Greek decent, which according to US racial categories is White.) I didn't know anyone who was Asian. My primary encounter with anything Asian came from the 1960s book *Tikki Tikki Tembo*, authored by a White woman with no understanding of Chinese culture or language.[30]

In the fourth grade I was given a solo in our class musical, *Sir Oliver's Song*, written to teach the Ten Commandments. The musical also assigned national identities to each song by way of musical flourishes, costumes, and vague cultural references. My song, it turned out, was the story of a Chinese boy who coveted what other people owned. My mom dutifully created a costume, including a hat made out of construction paper in the shape of a bamboo rice hat. I wore flip flops, stood in front of the class choir, put my palms together in a stereotypical posture of Asian subservience and sang my heart out.

Both of these experiences say a lot about my earliest racial formation in a context that bears a strong resemblance to the culture of White Christian nationalism. Racial discrimination, fear, and hatred are not habits created just out of intentional exclusion but also out of support for a status quo that has been deemed safe, protected, and good. Always good. So several years later, when a high school teacher joked in class that he "was going to find a wife in Hong Kong because the women there were more subservient," I thought of the comment as harmless.

White supremacy is insidious in large part because White racial identities are never marked. I learned in my all-white Christian school that I was the center of all that was known to be good. I had the right to safety and personal thriving. Being a Christian meant that I was right, which gave me the ability to cast judgment on those who were wrong. While I understood this privilege as part of my religious identity, I didn't understand that it was also part of my White racial identity.

When I began studying White racial identity as a seminary student, the analysis clicked in a part of my brain that had been longing to understand what in my early life had gone unspoken. I learned to see that White racial dominance is designed to show up in the most mundane ways, allowing its perpetrators plausible deniability. Studying evangelical purity culture has been an extended exercise in understanding White racial identity and how it has constructed White womanhood around gendered and racialized ideals that provide symbols and narratives of personal and collective innocence.

CHAPTER SEVEN

MYTHS AND MARTYRS OF WHITE CHRISTIAN NATIONALISM

THE HABITS OF being in a nation whose greatness is predicated on historical illiteracy and psychological defensiveness are formed through practices of ignorance. Historical illiteracy isn't a passive stance toward learning but an active resistance toward the truth and the cultivation of non-knowledge. Sociologist Jennifer Mueller describes this process as the development of racial ignorance, which creates the illusion that racial identity is irrelevant to one's lived experience.[1] Racial ignorance also means that racial inequality and histories of racist violence are non-factors when characterizing the collective and individual behaviors of US citizens. These practices have been normalized in the formation of White racial identity, a category that was constructed to indicate membership in a superior group with little to no qualifications beyond an affiliation with European ancestry and Christianity.

Ignorance is not the point, of course; innocence is: the desire to be free of guilt, released from responsibility, accountable only to one's own unfettered path to social, spiritual, and economic fulfillment. Protestant evangelicalism in the United States sanctified the practice of not-knowing and, like most of its attributes, was silently dispersed into the politics of national identity. Together, religious and national ambitions created a set of myths to promulgate collective innocence. According to historian Robin Bernstein, innocence is about capturing oblivion—the privilege to see nothing, do nothing, say nothing.[2] In common with Mueller's claims about ignorance, Bernstein writes, "This obliviousness was not merely an absence of knowledge, but an active state of repelling knowledge." "Holy ignorance," as she calls it, or the ability to perform "not-noticing" is also a trait associated with White children and women because of their presumed lack of or interest in sexual knowledge.

Innocence myths are premised upon disembodiment—the failure to ground ourselves in our own flesh and blood. Over generations these myths have reinforced a racial category that is both mysterious in its origins and relentless in its claims of superiority. Projects in disembodiment, such as color-evasion and sexual purity, allow us to persist in our ignorance even when the prophets among us call out their falsehood. In *The Fire Next Time*, James Baldwin writes of White Americans who cling to these innocence myths: "that [our] ancestors were all freedom-loving heroes, that they were born into the greatest country the world has ever seen, or that Americans are invincible in battle, wise in peace, that Americans have always dealt honorably with Mexicans and Indians and all other neighbors and inferiors, that American men are the world's most direct and virile, that American women are pure."[3]

For those of us raised within White evangelical purity culture, myths of innocence around our sexuality were prominent, obscuring the ways that we were also being socialized into the falsehoods of White racial identity. For former evangelicals recovering from purity culture, this means attending to various forms of disembodiment, sexual and racial. On social media, purity culture recovery sometimes appears as White women posing nude, in the bath with expensive champagne, and promoting self-help through dance, poetry, and movement. When these activities prioritize individual sexual well-being over collective justice, they fall into a performance of White feminism, a brand of female empowerment that prioritizes the needs of White women.

In November 2021, Brenda Davies, the host of the post-evangelical podcast *God Is Grey*, made this declaration on Instagram: "Purity culture parents, be warned: indoctrinating your daughters may cause religious trauma . . . wild self-acceptance & naked frolicking through the desert."[4] The post was based on an event Davies hosted at Joshua Tree National Park for a weekend of leisure and celebration. The group of women had publicly rejected purity culture, and though they represented a fraction of the post-purity movement, they all had public platforms and influencer status: podcasters, authors, actors, models, even a former beauty queen. Despite their proximity to prestige culture, the memoirs of two of the women present—Davies and Alice Greczyn—indicate that racial and class privilege do not exempt anyone from internalizing the belief that their bodies' needs and desires are in conflict with godly behavior. Not all the women present that weekend hold class and race privilege, nor did they all participate in the photo. But the photograph Davies posted, which included herself and Greczyn, reflected a class of women with access to many privileges, including close proximity to White beauty ideals, which reinforced the idea that only bodies with racial and aesthetic privilege can experience full recovery from sexual purity.

As a practice of disembodiment, purity culture teaches that our physical bodies and our need for sexual pleasure cannot be trusted. The body, according to these teachings, leads people to sin. Rejecting those desires offers the assurance of eternal salvation. White women who've departed purity culture often report experiences of disembodiment, including an inability to pursue their own sexual desires. In her memoir, *On Her Knees: Memoir of a Prayerful Jezebel*, Brenda Davies defines disembodiment as "believing the flesh to be evil and the heart deceitful."[5] For her, this meant asking God to save her from her own sexual desire or to send her a message that having sex was permissible. On her second date with the man she would eventually marry, she heard an answer: his roommate, also a Christian, had just had sex for the first time and had no regrets. At that revelation, Davies was able to relinquish her own commitment to sexual purity, as she now understood it impeded her body from embracing the pleasure God had designed it for.

In her memoir *Wayward: A Memoir of Spiritual Warfare and Sexual Purity*, Alice Greczyn describes how she discovered that her body held the key to her personal happiness. After rejecting Christianity for secular humanism, she found deep meaning in common physical pleasures that had been forbidden in her Christian family and community.

> I was taught to deny pleasures of the flesh . . . the physical, material world I was told to fear and abstain from was the very thing that made me want to live. Sex, food, drink, and nature. Music, dance, books, and kisses. Family, friends, animals, cuddles, and the belief-shattering salve of science. These were where I found peace and awe. These were where I found fulfillment and love.[6]

Like Davies and Greczyn, many in recovery from purity culture seek reconnection with their physical selves through mental health therapy, embodiment coaching, and sexual experimentation. However, the dilemma of disembodiment in purity culture is not simply about sexuality. It is also about race.

In the introduction to her memoir, Davies demonstrates a color-evasive ideology by asking, "How could I explain that whatever color, creed, sex, sexuality, religion—or lack thereof—you identify with, you might resonate with this book? The reason being, no matter how divided our life experience or ideology, there are universal themes—like fear, shame, and horniness (or the fear and shame that you never get horny)—that help us see one another."

In seeking to connect across various forms of difference, Davies claims that her experience taps into a universal understanding that "can bridge divides." To support her claim she draws upon the words of Dr. Martin Luther King Jr.: "Darkness cannot drive out darkness; only light can do that."[7] Davies continues, "When light is shined onto universal human experience—like love, sex, and relationships—we unify, not only with others, but within ourselves. We are meant to be whole." Her comments dismiss the possibility of racialized sexism, ignoring the fact that racism impacts all aspects of our lives, including our intimate relationships. By doing so, Davies remains informed by the color-evasive racism of her religious upbringing, focusing on unity, peace, and wholeness at the expense of a more accurate understanding of racial conflict. Unwittingly, she is performing another form of disembodiment, one afforded to all White people that allows us to ignore our own racial identity and privilege.

Prominent voices, such as those of Davies and Greczyn, champion a post-purity narrative that prioritizes sexual agency and liberation. But this narrative fails to acknowledge diverse experiences. Black women speaking about the history of resisting sexualized stereotypes, people with disabilities seeking visibility, or asexual people hoping to be treated with respect are excluded from a post-purity narrative that takes it cues from second-wave feminism.

Launched in the late 1960s, second-wave feminism failed to address the complexities of women's lived experiences by focusing solely on the needs of straight, White, middle-class women. The voices of queer women and women of color were suppressed as a threat to the movement, and feminist victories were marked by the expansion of White women's successes alone. Given these limitations, White second-wave feminism is a flawed example for post-purity healing as it excludes the embodied experiences of anyone whose needs and concerns extend beyond a narrow understanding of sexual liberation.

In her book *White Tears /Brown Scars: How White Feminism Betrays Women of Color*, scholar and journalist Ruby Hamad shows that the dilemmas of White womanhood are rooted in the brutal legacy of European settler-colonialism. "White society marked the bodies of women of color as a receptable for its sins so that it may claim innocence for itself, and, as the chosen symbol of the innocent perfection of whiteness, the white damsel with her tears of distress functions as both denial of and absolution for this violence."[8] Hamad examines how, in European colonies, White women were used to exonerate the entire colonial project as it claimed to bring civilization to the barbarous nations. In the United States, these same strategies became embedded in the project of sexual purity, offering White women security and status if they utilized their vulnerability to justify various forms of racist violence.

Using this historical framework, we can better understand the layered, embodied dilemmas of White women's recovery work from a religious system, such as the Southern Baptist Convention, that is, at present, deeply embroiled in a sexual abuse crisis and in its own refusal to reckon with its racist history and habits. In the same way that many Southern Baptist leaders fail to acknowledge the connections between the two, some post-purity advocates struggle to see evangelical purity culture as both a sexual and a racial project. Without careful, critical engagement into how purity culture impacts White women's racial habits, we risk replicating similar harms. Our bodies are trained for racial comfort and demand it as a form of personal wellness, empowerment, or holiness, depending on context.

A month after Davies posted the group photo from Joshua Tree, she began receiving criticism from some of her followers. They noted that the women's expression of bodily self-acceptance was achievable only because they reflected White beauty ideals. Another follower noted that she had been sitting in great discomfort with the photo for similar reasons: it did not reflect a thoughtful engagement with various forms of privilege, nor did it address the racial segregation that exists within post-purity recovery efforts.

Though the criticisms were offered with support and even celebration of the group's activities, Davies defended herself, intimating to her audience that as the mother of a vulnerable child (her toddler was sick at the time), people should extend her grace by minimizing their criticism. She deflected any call to confront the complex issues her followers raised, issues common in spaces where White women and women of color exchange ideas about liberating our bodies. The ability to shield oneself from painful accountability is a racial habit of White womanhood. This is referred to pejoratively as "White women's tears" because of how frequently the people who are harmed by White women have to console those same women, who use their gender-based vulnerability to plead innocence to wrongdoing.[9] Davies's response reinforced the White woman's privilege to assert her own racial innocence in order to maintain the illusion of moral goodness.

Greczyn, on the other hand, was not interested in vulnerability and penned a blog post to vent her frustration with Davies's followers' call to accountability. In the post, titled "The Photo: How a Girls' Getaway in Joshua Tree Became a Symbol of White Supremacy and Why I'm Not Here to Do Better," Greczyn initially articulated the critiques with clarity: "Our photo sent a silent message: You must *still* be a beautiful, white, and able-bodied woman to represent an ideal of *deconstructed* purity culture. In this way, our photo symbolized the continued upholding of white Christian supremacy in post-Christian spaces."[10] She astutely identified why people would object to the picture. Despite this, she went on to claim that while these criticisms were understandable, they were invalid. Greczyn leapt into an attack on "woke culture," which she believes uses shaming tactics akin to those of her evangelical upbringing. "We were shamed for being light-skinned. We were shamed for appearing able-bodied. We were shamed for being attractive. We were shamed because I am not curvy, because Brenda is not Black, and because Sophia is not visibly disabled. If we were these, the shame would not have been hurled our way." She goes on to denounce cancel culture as a secular form of the over-reaching, religious accountability she experienced in her early life. "Know what I think you really hate us for?" she writes. "Beauty privilege."

She is correct—this is exactly what her critics were saying. Beauty is a racialized construct that exploits women by making us believe that our primary responsibility is to maintain our beauty or seek to achieve this amorphous ideal at all costs. Its power sits at the very nexus of misogyny, White supremacy, and ableism. The problem is not a person or photograph that approximates or achieves this ideal, but an uncritical investment in its power.

Understanding one's mixed-race identity in the US racial landscape is a lot of work, especially given the insufficiency of our racial categories. Everyone has the right to pursue their understanding in their own time and way. But Greczyn dismissed her own mixed-race background and belittled the topic altogether, fully rejecting the criticisms of women of color asking her and other members of their group to consider the overall impact of the photo's racial representation. Though she raises thoughtful questions in the midst of her anger, Greczyn displays a form of racial fragility that is especially manifest among White and White-passing women who struggle to understand what it means to hold multiple social identities, some that confer privilege and others that designate vulnerability.

What's most telling in Greczyn's post is her brief nod to the issue of race: "I am as Korean as I am French, with so many other ethnicities mingling in my blood that to name them all would be boring. I will write more in the future on the topic of being mixed race and ethnically ambiguous. For now, my personal reckoning with my racial identity is still too fresh to share. Yeah blah yeah, light-skinned privilege and all that, go ahead, school me like I haven't heard it before."

Sexual purity holds a racist legacy that many White and White-passing women raised in evangelical purity culture were never taught to acknowledge. In our color-evasive White churches, we learned to be obedient and demure, always deferring to adults in power. Today, some former evangelicals engage in robust conversations about the failure of White evangelicalism to address racism and how our experiences have been shaped by racial privilege and White supremacy. Sexual liberation is only one thread in a tapestry of collective freedom that includes a necessary examination of how White supremacy informs our claims to sexual healing. Interrogating how we, as survivors of sexual and/or religious harm, remain tied to systems of privilege and oppression allows us to find healing from our own racial habits. More importantly, it allows us to see how Whiteness intercepts our desires for clarity and compassion, distorting them into hardened ideologies and White-saviorism.

The rejection of and recovery from purity culture requires us to engage with intersecting forms of privilege and oppression. For White and White-passing women, this means understanding that efforts to achieve idealized versions of ourselves are not just projects in self-enhancement but in maintaining the White racial privilege we've been trained to ignore. Being able to experience sexual pleasure after years of sex-negative indoctrination can be an act of resistance. But acts of resistance extracted from a historical understanding of sexual purity's racist legacy reinforces the racial segregation of post-purity efforts, making it arduous for women of color to achieve the same. Though leaving evangelicalism and purity culture may offer White women opportunities for achieving personal and sexual fulfillment, that does not equate to sexual, gender, or racial justice. The critics of the Joshua Tree photo have taught us something important: the dilemma of White womanhood is that we have inherited the inability to see beyond our own well-being. Recovery from purity culture and its supporting ideologies is a multifaceted project that requires attention to the historical and religious formation of our sexual *and* racial embodiment.

When we shift away from the hyper-individualistic frame of Whiteness, we can see the broader cultural trends and religious movements that animated evangelical purity culture. The sexual purity movement of the 1990s and early 2000s that these (and thousands of other) women revolted against was first and foremost an expression of White Christian nationalism. It was rooted in the need to represent the American nation-state as inherently innocent, embodying a special relationship with God since its founding. Beginning in the nineteenth century, various groups have symbolized this innocence, representations drawn from the racialized history of White evangelicalism, which asserts the White evangelical family unit as the foundation for a strong Christian America. White women, sexually pure teenagers, and fetuses in the womb have all at some point been used to signify the myth of national innocence and to elicit demands for increased White, evangelical political power and social influence.

On January 6, 2021, the displays of White Christian nationalism in the nation's capital further reinforced this symbolic power, in particular that of White womanhood. Stories and images of White women attacking the Capitol confounded many people, including the women themselves. Accounts by and about these women roundly presented them as innocent of wrongdoing and even of being subject to wrongdoing. The symbolic power of White womanhood is deeply embedded into the genetic makeup of the United States in such a way that conflict between the two is unimaginable.

There are many examples of White women, followers of Trump, using claims of innocence to exonerate themselves and their MAGA savior in the wake of the January 6 insurrection. For these women, Trump's loss in the 2020 presidential election was a spiritual dilemma: if God had anointed him to remake the nation according to traditional (i.e., White Christian) values, why had God abandoned the plan? The existential and constitutional crisis that ensued demonstrated just how easily Trump and his team were able to manipulate White Christians into acknowledging him as God's anointed. And when called to avenge the injustice, they showed up.

Among the people arrested and charged for participating in the Capitol insurrection were 102 White women. According to the report

The Women of January 6th, produced by the Program on Extremism, at George Washington University, 33 of those women faced felony charges and 66 faced misdemeanor charges.[11] The report describes how women play a unique role in far-right organizations, one it describes as based on "traditional gender roles" that characterize White women as innately nurturing, virtuous, moral, and innocent. Though the report authors are more interested in the women's crimes than in their relational status, they note how the women of January 6 were represented by their lawyers as caregivers and by their relationship to male authority.

The report found that women in far-right organizations are especially good in conducting public relations because they offer a "softer" presentation of the group's goals. By leaning into these feminine traits, women lend their "good reputations" to the movement. White women in the contemporary US have these good reputations for the same reasons they did in the nineteenth century: they use their racial power and maternal authority to support male-dominated hierarchies. In short, their good reputations allow them to forward very disreputable ideologies.

Gina Bisignano, a cosmetologist from Beverly Hills, California, was arrested and indicted for her participation in the January 6 insurrection. At her arraignment she pled not guilty to all charges, including obstruction of an official proceeding, civil disorder, and engaging in physical violence in a restricted building. But video footage showed Bisignano during the insurrection with a bullhorn directing people to bring their weapons inside. "We need strong, angry patriots to help our boys, they don't want to leave. We need protection. [. . .] We the people are not going to take it anymore. You are not going to take away our Trumpy Bear, you are not going to take away our votes and our freedom that I thank God for. This is 1776 and we the people will never give up. We will never let our country go globalist. George Soros, you can go to hell."[12]

Despite evidence of her guilt, Bisignano insisted on her innocence multiple times. She described her involvement in the insurrection as a passive one to her local newspaper, the *Beverly Hills Courier.* "I was caught up, I was scared, I was excited. A guy said to say that over the megaphone. I don't even remember saying it." She complained that reviewers on her business's Yelp page were characterizing her as a terrorist, to which she responded, "I want to clear my name. Everyone in Beverly Hills knows I'm not—I am a Christian." Following up with a final declaration, "I didn't do anything."[13]

Bisignano's cognitive dissonance around her involvement in the insurrection continued into her sentencing. Initially pleading not guilty, she eventually signed a plea deal because of her fear of a long-term prison sentence. And yet, with other Trump supporters, she maintains her belief that her actions that day were just.

Shortly after the chaos had ended on January 6, Fox News host Tucker Carlson came on the air and expressed his confusion over Ashli Babbitt, the White woman shot and killed by Capitol Police as she attempted to trespass into the building. Carlson (who initially referred to the thirty-six-year-old Babbitt as a girl), said, "Why did the woman go to the rally in the first place? We do not know anything about her, but she did not look particularly radical. She bears no resemblance to the angry children we have seen wrecking our cities . . . pasty, entitled, reckless nihilists, setting fires, spray-painting slogans on statues. She didn't look like that. The woman in the capital hallway pretty much looked like everyone else. Why was she there?"[14]

On right-wing discussion boards, Babbitt was lauded as "an innocent girl" and a martyr. She quickly became a form of propaganda, another White woman used as a "tool that softens the edges of the far right," according to journalist Seyward Darby.[15]

What Bisignano's and Babbitt's stories demonstrate is that White women's innocence is a powerful mythology that shapes national ideologies about race, sexuality, and national survival and security. Whether White women deploy this trope in moments of personal crisis, White Christian nationalism allows them the right and even responsibility to do so. Through White women's presumed vulnerability, sexual purity, and religious piety, White Christian nationalists uphold myths of the nation's White racial innocence wherein anti-Black and other forms of state-sanctioned violence are premised as protective, rather than aggressive. In other words, Christian nationalism requires that the US nation-state propagates White women's incontrovertible moral authority in order to exonerate both the United States and Christianity from a long-standing history of racial violence.

The 2021 assault on the US Capitol was a violent defense of myths of national innocence. Racial reckonings around anti-Blackness created alarm among White people invested in myths of post-racialism. The Capitol insurrection was, in part, a reclamation of White power, with White women available to remind us that Blackness itself represents criminality and Whiteness innocence. Jenna Ryan, another White woman present that day, summed it up best in a now-infamous tweet: "Definitely not going to jail. Sorry I have blonde hair White skin a great job a great future and I'm not going to jail. Sorry to rain on your hater parade. I did nothing wrong."[16] In fact, eight months later, Ryan was sentenced to sixty days in jail after pleading guilty to one count of parading, demonstrating, or picketing in the Capitol.

The ideology of sexual purity is a powerful one that has secured White women's reputation for innocence, and in doing so, it has offered White women access to a unique form of racial power that can be utilized on the national stage. Whether we elect to deploy this racial power, the United States has always acknowledged White womanhood as a national asset that protects White racial power.

Far-right extremist groups and actions have increased significantly since the election of our first Black president, in 2008. But tropes about White womanhood exist across the political spectrum and appear in much more mundane ways. These tropes socialize young White women and girls into a world where our value is marked by being perceived as innocent and vulnerable, and we are rewarded when we play these roles. It's for our sake that most sex education is nothing more than lessons laced with sexual fear and anxiety. In evangelical churches and families, sex is presented as dangerous to girls who must work overtime to protect themselves from male sexuality, while at the same time being tasked with controlling male sexuality.

Sexual fear in the United States is not race neutral. Learning to fear sex and sexuality is learning to believe that what Ida B. Wells called the lynching myth is true. Sexual fear does not exist without fear of the racial other. This is why the Southern Baptist Convention teaches its young people to wait for true love but also fails to adequately address the problem of systemic racism. This is why right-wing groups point to the security and innocence of White children to justify the erasure of Black history and the truth of this nation's violent past.

Evangelical purity culture has left in its wake a spectrum of harm that includes religious trauma, sexual shame, an inability to have or enjoy sex, sexual abuse, and rape. But underneath all those object lessons about chewed gum, crushed cookies, and toothpaste—euphemisms for an impure life—is something even more sinister about our collective national past. In the United States, purity and impurity have always been racially coded. To be White is to be free and pure. To not be White is to be suspect and impure. Purity culture didn't just form us sexually; it formed us racially. If you listen to people of color who grew up in purity culture in a White church, you see this very clearly. Seek out those people on social media and in books and articles and listen to their stories.

Sexual purity taught us something about being White. And for those of us who are White women, it taught us that the preservation of our purity entitles us to a racial power that keeps us invested in the United States as a White Christian nation.

CONCLUSION

AFTER ROE

EVANGELICAL PURITY CULTURE comprises mythologies of inno-cence that have shaped Americans' expectations for family, sexuality, and gender identity. It asserts that these myths are essential to na-tional prosperity and security because they assure the nation's special relationship to God. The United States as a nation is deeply invested in innocence myths in large part because White evangelicals have exploited these narratives for their own political gain. Evangelical purity culture is the focus of this book, but it is not even the most pronounced effort to activate innocence myths.

As an evangelical teenager, I attended the March for Life with a group from my Christian high school every year from 1989 to 1992. In my senior year, I organized the trip after being tapped for the job by a classmate who had previously held the position. Being selected was itself a status upgrade in my small, parent-run school, one that paid out later in the year when I was recognized with an award for "servant-leadership." My mother volunteered for a local pro-life hot-line and bought me a tiny silver pin shaped like two small feet, the size of a fetus at five weeks, which I wore often. My father, a local pastor who previously chaired our counties anti-porn campaign, ac-companied my mother to numerous demonstrations. Between school and family there was never any question that being a Christian meant opposing abortion, pornography, and comprehensive sex education— all presumed threats to my personal well-being.

When *Roe v. Wade* was overturned in June 2022, I found myself revisiting these experiences within the pro-life movement. I remember feeling the electricity of conflict as I watched Roman Catholics wield giant posters of aborted fetuses and counter-protestors wave wire coat hangers. The number of young people, including children younger than me, created the atmosphere of an ecumenical church picnic but with political stakes. We were in our nation's capital to assert an unwavering belief that opposing abortion was a biblical mandate (as numerous signs reminded), one of many that we believed offered superior guidance for individual and national decision-making.

I believed my Christian faith was a David facing the Goliath of secularism and selfish women. I had been strategically recruited by the right to life movement bent on using the innocence of youth to perpetuate an ideology connecting sexual, racial, and national innocence. I didn't know that twenty-five years earlier White evangelicals did not even consider abortion a political or religious issue, and that many clergy assisted women with procuring the procedure even when it was illegal. It was physicians who first started campaigning for legalization as they watched the numbers of illegal abortions increase over the course of the twentieth century. When *Roe* was first instated, public support for legal abortion was well above 64 percent.[1]

It is helpful to think about evangelical purity culture and the pro-life movement as sharing a set of habits and practices that govern White Christian nationalistic ideals of family, gender, and marriage. These, of course, predate the fundamentalist takeover of the Southern Baptist Church and the emergence of the religious right in the late 1970s, which many view as the origin point for the evangelical pro-life movement. These ideals are rooted in a nineteenth-century gendered and racial order in which social and political power was limited to White, Protestant men and, increasingly, a few White Protestant women. Today, religious leaders and their followers, along with elected officials, willfully confuse these nineteenth-century ideals of gender, marriage, and family with "biblical values" in order to assert them as universal norms and virtues.

White Christian nationalism endorses a culture in which virtue is performed through disembodiment, a skill that White evangelical adolescent girls are especially encouraged to excel in. In purity culture, *disembodiment* means ignoring the physical prompts of our bodies, as confirmed by a growing body of literature on eating disorders among White evangelical women.[2] But it also means learning to ignore the ways that our sexual, gender, and racial identities point to a past that is anything but innocent. The most prominent form of racism in the United States is not that perpetrated by extremists but by White moderates, liberals even, who are unable and unwilling to address racial identity and racial violence and have distorted that failure into a virtue. For White evangelicals and other Christians, the virtue of color-evasive racism is distinctly religious.

Fears of a changing racial and sexual order in the late 1970s would allow conservative activists the opportunity to align White evangelicalism with the Republican Party. The driving concerns of many White evangelicals who helped elect Ronald Reagan president focused on the increased opportunity of public assistance for people of color. While White people had long benefited from federal assistance (housing loans, the GI Bill, widows' pensions), public sentiment toward assistance shifted dramatically as more people of color sought and received the same. Reagan's rhetoric, which conservative White evangelicals accepted with little question, presumed that "undeserving" people exploited the welfare system, this word being code for women having children "out of wedlock" in order to be eligible for welfare benefits.

When Reagan began campaigning for president in the 1970s, he helped galvanize White anxiety by describing the kind of person who exploited the welfare system. He described a woman named Linda

Taylor, whom Chicago newspapers dubbed "the welfare queen."[3] Taylor was by all accounts a criminal mastermind. She attempted to kidnap children from hospitals for ransom and left a trail of suspicious deaths behind her. She was guilty of many things, but when arrested in 1974 the primary charge brought against her was welfare fraud.[4] Though Taylor committed crimes that deserved consequences, politicians' and the media's portrayal of her as a typical welfare recipient was at best inaccurate and at worst racist and classist propaganda. Because of Reagan, the welfare queen stereotype became a staple of US political and economic rhetoric. She was a poor woman of color who used her reproductive capacity to have as many children as possible so she could collect even more money from the government. Today the welfare queen myth remains a powerful one despite the fact that Taylor's claim to this title has been fully debunked.

My adolescence was shaped by expectations of self-sufficiency and self-determination. Anything valuable in my life had to be something I achieved through hard work and personal discipline. My young life was shaped by a series of exercises dedicated to self-containment and bodily control, practices I now recognize as forming my White racial identity. Being "good" meant taking personal responsibility and accepting the consequences of my actions, so I learned how to avoid consequences altogether by attaching my self-worth to sexual purity.

What I once considered my faith practices were in fact efforts to conform to the virtues of a White, Christian America. Disguised as personal piety in my adolescent development, my opposition to abortion, premarital sex, and comprehensive sex education were part of a strategy to enhance the political power of White evangelicals.

The goal of White Christian nationalism as a movement is to bring all levels of social organization—the individual, the family, the church, and the nation—under a single standard of Christian morality. The rhetoric of "parental rights" and "family values" is steeped in these same innocence myths, creating a set of virtues based on an idealized view of White, middle-class family life. Today, "parental rights" is being used to challenge the teaching of African American history, with the claim that it is harmful to White children to learn that their nation does not have an innocent past. White racial identity has been formed in the United States to deflect responsibility, through the cultivation of ignorance and under the guise of adhering to the virtue of innocence. The same argument used to miseducate young people about US history is the same used by social conservatives against sex education, including discussions of gender identity. Whiteness is the power to erase the past and its consequences, to ignore the reality of bodies and the assertion of their needs. Ultimately, it is the power to erase the sexual, racial, and religious diversity that is a vital feature of American democracy.

Since the end of *Roe*, I've been reflecting on my own reproductive choices, which include an IUD and a bed I am pleased to share only with my fourteen-pound Chug, Gibson. I have never had an overwhelming urge to become pregnant, give birth, or parent. Throughout my thirties I held the question lightly, thinking that I should remain open to the possibility just in case I was destined for marriage and motherhood (spoiler: I am not). When two friends and one family member began making serious plans to parent on their own, I realized this was not a priority for me. "I'd rather write a book," I told my friend, a rabbi now serving a congregation in Minneapolis. My own internalized misogyny had convinced me that while I could have both a family and a career, I could never do both well. Therefore, in order to feel and be successful, I had to make a choice.

Two years later, Rabbi Tamar would select a sperm donor and eventually welcome her daughter, Sophie, into her life. With a supportive congregation she found the resources, acceptance, and welcome for her daughter, who became a beloved member of the community. Along the way I marveled at her certainty. How did she know this is what she wanted? How did she know she'd have what she needed to be a single mom and a full-time religious leader? How would she deal with the raised eyebrows and accusatory whispers? Or possible attempts to have her removed from her position? But then I realized, she wasn't an evangelical Christian. She wasn't conditioned to limit the domain of her authority and expertise to motherhood, like I was. And her faith tradition did not stigmatize single-motherhood, as mine did, but offered a variety of reproductive options and support, including abortion access.

White Christian nationalism is dripping with misogyny, the kind that demands perfectionism from women, especially those who aspire to motherhood. The perfectionism of Christian motherhood, taught to me as a sacrificial vocation, required the purest intentions and the stoutest of resolve. Mothering is where White women demonstrate our superiority. I knew this instinctively. I also knew I would be miserable spending a lifetime working to achieve this ideal. Mothering is a competitive sport, especially in White, religious communities. It encourages the kind of perfectionism that is meant to exhibit the racial superiority of White families.

In my youth, Christian motherhood was held up as a White, middle-class ideal, with mothers praised for self-sacrifice, obedient children, and a family sustained through self-sufficiency. Though many White people relied on public support and services (including mine), the political rhetoric of the early 1980s depicted black women's hypersexuality as the cause of their dependency on public resources. I learned to be the opposite: sexually pure, sacrificial, and self-sufficient. I knew my value was good only if I were contained by the virtues of moral motherhood. Of course, I was not a mother, but I was part of a White evangelical community shaped by racist ideologies that used my virtue to signal its own superiority.

Today, the evangelical pro-life movement remains fervent in its assertion that banning abortion will restore the nation to its pristine condition. Because of this, the efforts and presence of young, White women remains vital. White women's sexual and racial identities in the pro-life movement are formed around a politics of moral motherhood. Reinvented by the religious right to denigrate women who did not or could not achieve the goals of self-sufficiency and sexual purity, the moral motherhood of the pro-life movement uses false and blatantly racist stereotypes to secure White women's racial power and political influence. Within conservative evangelical communities, women have limited autonomy, the pro-life movement being the one place where they can exhibit their power over others, particularly those who do not conform to the identity politics of White Christian nationalism. Rhetoric from abortion opponents urges people to "protect the innocent unborn." But in practice, the pro-life movement provides White women in conservative religious communities access to racial power and political influence that they would not have otherwise.

The innocence myths of the United States have proven to be unsustainable, as failures of truth usually are. Dismantling their infrastructure requires us to demand access to our unvarnished past, a bold commitment to truth-telling, and an openness to sitting in nuance and contradiction. The backlash against reproductive rights, historical education, and the increased expansion of civil rights for people of all races, religions, sexualities, and genders is expected in an increasingly authoritarian society. But resistance to this backlash is coming from multiple fronts, as many invested in bodily autonomy draw upon numerous historical precedents that show how embodied resistance can shift us back toward a thriving democracy. If we have learned anything from the pursuit of purity and the illusions it perpetuates, it's that our bodies—the physical manifestations that we present in the world—are not simply matter. They also matter to the way we are situated within national mythologies of religion, race, and sexuality.

ACKNOWLEDGMENTS

WHEN MY FIRST BOOK, *Virgin Nation: Sexual Purity and American Adolescence*, was published in 2015, I was unprepared for the response from readers outside my academic circles. The interest from journalists, bloggers, podcasters, and mental health professionals challenged my assumptions about who I was writing for and I soon began to shift my academic work toward more public-facing projects. If (and it was a big if) I were to write a second book on evangelical purity culture, I needed to listen to the stories of those impacted by purity culture. And I needed money in order to secure time away from my teaching responsibilities.

I am first and foremost most grateful for two generous grants from the Louisville Institute and the Luce Foundation's Religion and Sexual Abuse Project, especially for the cohorts of scholars I was able to join and the individuals whose work and lives continue to inspire and console me, particularly Kent Brintnall, Mark Clatterbuck, Ann Gleig, Amanda Lucia, Jorge Rodríguez, and Nicole Symmonds.

As a lecturer at my institution, I am not eligible for a research sabbatical, but these grants allowed me to buy my own sabbatical in the 2019–2020 school year and launch the After Purity Project, an interview study focused on people who had grown up and out of evangelical purity culture. I was deeply uncertain if people would want to talk to me about their experiences in purity culture during a global pandemic, but I was very wrong. Over 160 people signed up to participate, with 65 agreeing to sit for an interview. To those individuals who shared their stories so openly with me, I have the deepest gratitude. Many had told their stories before, working through religious trauma and sexual and other anxieties with mental health professionals, friends, partners, and other compassionate listeners. Others were very much in the thick of their anger and confusion. While these were the most difficult interviews to conduct, they taught me to recognize and understand the debilitating effects of religious and family-based trauma. Each interviewee taught me how to listen and how to build community around shared desires for new ways of being.

During my research I was contacted by two young scholars working on their own projects investigating the impacts of purity culture. A few months later, Liv Schultz and Tessi Muskrat started the Purity Culture Research Collective (PCRC), creating a space and community for researchers, artists, and mental health professionals to share their work with one another. Together with Kathryn House (my intrepid co-editor) Lauren Sawyer, Victoria House, MiHee Kim-Cort, Rebecca Wolf, Rebekah Vickery, Melissa Payne, Jenny McGrath, and Elizabeth Gish, we have published a special issue of the *Journal of Theology and Sexuality*. The collective work of this group, one unaffiliated with any academic institution, has been nothing short of astounding. When I made the decision midway through the writing of this book to move on from studying evangelical purity culture, I had no hesitations given the work and commitments of the members of the PCRC.

Shifting toward public-facing work can be risky in a field in which status comes via our affiliations with academic institutions, and only the rare few rise to prominence. Among those who have are Bradley Onishi and Daniel Miller, both former evangelical youth ministers turned religion professors turned podcast hosts of *Straight White American Jesus*. When they contacted me about my work on purity culture, I only had one word for them: yes. Their generosity with their

platform, desire for collaboration, and ambition to educate everyone about White Christian nationalism was the shot of adrenaline
I needed to recognize and move toward my own goals. With them
I taught the seminar Sexual Purity and Dis/Embodiment, which
became a workshop of ideas with brilliant thinkers also seeking to
understand the political and cultural significance of evangelical purity
culture. After three years of Brad asking, "Sara, when are you going
to make a podcast on purity culture?" I did the thing, and I'm so glad
I did. Working with Brad, Scott Okomoto, and Kari Onishi of Axis
Mundi Media was the best crash course in podcast production one
could ask for. Learning to write podcast scripts was the single most
helpful process for learning how to translate my academic thoughts
into accessible and compelling storytelling.

My week with the Religion and Democracy Lab at the University
of Virginia was especially helpful for understanding how public-facing
work, podcast production, and activist scholarship sit together quite
comfortably. Seeing my academic colleagues expand into more creative ventures has been a great source of joy. When it came time for
my own, it was like taking deep gulps of clean fresh air into my newly
expanded lungs. My podcast (available wherever you get yours), *Pure
White: Sexual Purity and White Supremacy*, helped shape the through-
line of this book.

Early drafts of this book were read and heard by a group of people
whose friendships have become a bulwark against the sharp edges
of life. Dawn Burns, Sarah Carson, Audrey Clare Farley, Linda Kay
Klein, Bex Miller, Sarah Stankorb, Glenn Taylor, and Cait West are
all writers of poetry, creative nonfiction, and fiction whose work holds
me in awe. Early in my interviews, I noticed an overwhelming theme:
disembodiment. Traditional academic writing requires the author
to remain removed from the pages, as if the absence conveys some
authority from on high. To maintain this voice felt like a betrayal of
my integrity, and so I began considering the ways I could show up

in these pages. Learning to write creative nonfiction and then being asked to read that work in front of people was a seismic shift in my self-understanding as a writer. Together, Dawn, Cait, Sarah, and I have become experts in trauma-informed, compassionate storytelling that provides people a soft place to sit and listen to one another. Writing and reading about religious and sexual trauma is a task I would never attempt with anyone else, but with them it has become as necessary as breathing.

It took me years to feel confident about myself as a nonacademic writer, to be attuned to the places in my body (not my head) where truths that needed airing lay in wait. In 2024, I applied for and attended my first nonfiction writing workshop, organized by S. B. Plate-Rodriguez of the Association for Public Religion and Intellectual Life and run by Brooke Wilensky-Lanford. I am incredibly grateful for their ability to create a temporary community that affirmed my hopes that I could write from my whole self, not just a disembodied brain.

Keeping faith in any book project is work. Having people walk alongside you during the process makes all the difference. Much gratitude to my literary agent David Morris at Hyponymous Literary for teaching me so much about the publishing industry and helping me find the best home for this project. Deepest thanks to my colleague Dr. Samira Mehtha for introducing me to Amy Caldwell at Beacon Press and to Amy for her guidance and feedback on the manuscript. Your enthusiasm for the work has helped calm any remaining fears I had about breaking the fourth wall of academic writing. I have been reading books published by Beacon Press since I started my graduate education, so to be able to count myself among their authors feels like finding a home I didn't realize I was looking for.

This book is the product of a lot of luck (as nothing happens in the academic world without it), learning to hold all things loosely, and seeking to speak a truth that resonates for both the individual and the collective. An empathic massage therapist once told me that

I have the support I need, even when I don't feel it. That I am surrounded by colleagues, friends, and family who provide that support is a tangible fact. I have numerous concentric circles of support that I often fail to recognize. If I were to name them all here, it would be an embarrassment of riches. But they are each present in this book, if not in name, then in the spirit of growing together into something new.

FURTHER READING

Allison, Emily Joy. *#ChurchToo: How Purity Culture Upholds Abuse and How to Find Healing*. Minneapolis: Broadleaf Books, 2021.

Anderson, Dianna. *Damaged Goods: New Perspectives on Christian Purity*. New York: Jericho Books, 2015.

Anderson, Laura. *When Religion Hurts: Healing from Religious Trauma and the Impact of High-Control Religion*. Grand Rapids, MI: Brazos Press, 2023.

Baldwin, James. *The Fire Next Time*. New York: Penguin Random House, 1962.

Bederman, Gail. *Manliness and Civilization: A Cultural History of Gender and Race in the United States*. Chicago: University of Chicago Press, 1996.

Bernstein, Robin. *Racial Innocence: Performing American Childhood from Slavery to Civil Rights*. New York: New York University Press, 2011.

Bjork-James, Sophie. *The Divine Institution: White Evangelicalism's Politics of the Family*. New Brunswick, NJ: Rutgers University Press, 2021.

Botham, Fay. *"Almighty God Created the Races": Christianity, Interracial Marriage, and American Law*. Durham: University of North Carolina Press, 2013.

Brown, Christa. *Baptistland: A Memoir of Abuse, Betrayal, and Transformation*. Grand Rapids, MI: Lake Drive Books, 2024.

Butler, Anthea. *White Evangelical Racism: The Politics of Morality in America*. Chapel Hill: University of North Carolina Press, 2021.

Chastain, Blake. *Exvangelical and Beyond: How American Christianity Went Radical and the Movement That's Fighting Back*. New York: TarcherPerigree, 2024.

Cheng, Anne Anlin. *Ornamentalism*. New York: Oxford University Press, 2021.

Cooper, Brittney. *Eloquent Rage: How a Black Feminist Found Her Super-power*. New York: St. Martin's Press, 2018.

Curtiss, Jesse. *The Myth of Colorblind Christians: Evangelicals and White Supremacy in the Civil Rights Era*. New York: New York University Press, 2021.

Douglas, Kelly B. *Sexuality and the Black Church: A Womanist Perspective*. New York: Orbis Book, 1999.

Feagin, Joe. *The White Racial Frame: Centuries of Racial Framing and Counter-Framing*, 3rd ed. New York: Routledge, 2020.

Grant, Jacquelyn. *White Women's Christ, Black Women's Jesus: Feminist Christology and Black Women's Response*. Atlanta: Scholars Press, 1989.

Hamad, Ruby. *White Tears/Brown Scars: How White Feminism Betrays Women of Color*. New York: Catapult Press, 2020.

Harris, Shannon. *The Woman They Wanted: Shattering the Illusion of the Good Christian Wife*. Minneapolis: Broadleaf Books, 2023.

Haynes, Stephen. *Noah's Curse: The Biblical Justification of American Slavery*. Oxford: Oxford University Press, 2002.

Higginbotham, Evelyn Brooks. *Righteous Discontent: The Women's Movement in the Black Baptist Church, 1880–1920*. Cambridge, MA: Harvard University Press, 1994.

Hodes, Martha. *White Women and Black Men: Illicit Sex in the 19th-Century South*. New Haven, CT: Yale University Press, 1999.

Jackson, Olivia. *(Un)Certain: A Collective Memoir of Deconstructing Faith*. London: SCM Press, 2023.

Jacobs, Harriet. *Incidents in the Life of a Slave Girl, Written by Herself*. Edited by L. Maria Child. Boston: Published for the Author, 1861. https://www.gutenberg.org/ebooks/11030.

Klein, Linda Kay. *Pure: Inside the Movement that Shamed a Generation of Women and How I Broke Free*. New York: Atria Press, 2018.

McCammon, Sarah. *The Exvangelicals: Loving, Living, and Leaving the White Evangelical Church*. New York: St. Martin's Press, 2024.

McCleneghan, Bromleigh. *Good Christian Sex: Why Chastity Isn't the Only Option and Other Things the Bible Says About Sex*. New York: Harper One, 2016.

Mitchell, Michelle. *Righteous Propagation: African Americans and the Politics of Racial Destiny After Reconstruction*. Durham: University of North Carolina Press, 2004.

Moultrie, Monique. *Passionate and Pious: Religious Media and Black Women's Sexuality*. Durham, NC: Duke University Press, 2017.

Mueller, Jennifer. "Racial Ideology or Racial Ignorance? An Alternative Theory of Racial Ignorance." *Sociological Theory* 38, no. 2 (May 19, 2020).

Onishi, Bradley. *Preparing for War: The Extremist History of White Christian Nationalism—and What Comes Next.* Minneapolis: Broadleaf Books, 2023.

Painter, Nell Irvin. *The History of White People.* New York: W.W. Norton, 2010.

Rogers, Frank, Jr. *Cradled in the Arms of Compassion: A Spiritual Journal from Trauma to Recovery.* Grand Rapids, MI: Lake Drive Books, 2023.

Sharlet, Jeff. *The Undertow: Scenes from a Slow Civil War.* New York: W. W. Norton, 2023.

Snow, Jennifer. "The Civilization of White Men: The Race of the Hindu in the *United States v. Bhagat Singh Thind.*" In *Race, Nation and Religion in the Americas,* edited by Elizabeth McAlister and Henry Goldschmidt. New York: Oxford University Press, 2004.

Stankorb, Sarah. *Disobedient Women: How a Small Group of Faithful Women Exposed Abuse, Brought Down Powerful Pastors, and Ignited an Evangelical Reckoning.* Nashville: Worthy Press, 2023.

Stroop, Chrissy, and Lauren O'Neal. *Empty the Pews: Stories of Leaving the Church.* Indianapolis: Epiphany Publishing, 2019.

Wells, Ida B. *Southern Horrors and Other Writings: The Anti-Lynching Campaign of Ida B. Wells, 1892–1900.* Edited by Jacqueline Jones Royster. New York: Bedford/St. Martin's, 1997.

NOTES

INTRODUCTION

1. Anthony Petro, *After the Wrath of God: AIDS, Sexuality, and American Religion* (Oxford: Oxford University Press, 2015), 78, 83.

2. Sean McDowell, "Purity Culture, True Love Waits and More: A Conversation with Richard Ross," February 1, 2021, https://www.youtube.com/watch?v=B-cP2i_XgJE.

3. Sharaya Colter, "True Love Waits Returns to Where It Started," https://www.baptistpress.com/resource-library/news/true-love-waits-returns-to-where-it-began-20-years-ago/.

4. Quotes from Sara Moslener, *Virgin Nation: Sexual Purity and American Adolescence* (New York: Oxford University Press, 2015), 118.

5. Carly Tennes, "Why Nearly Every 2000s Disney Channel Star Wore a Purity Ring," Cracked.com, January 25, 2022, https://www.cracked.com/article_32395_why-nearly-every-2000s-disney-channel-star-wore-a-purity-ring.html.

6. Donna Freitas, *Sex and the Soul: Juggling Spirituality, Sexuality, Romance, and Religion on America's College Campuses* (Oxford: Oxford University Press, 2008).

7. Alexis Shotwell, *Against Purity: Living Ethically in Compromised Times* (Minneapolis: University of Minnesota Press, 2016), 37.

CHAPTER ONE: THE PURITY MYTH

1. Linda Kay Klein, *Pure: Inside the Evangelical Movement That Shamed a Generation of Young Women and How I Broke Free* (New York: Touchstone, 2018), 3.

2. Names of all research participants have been changed to maintain confidentiality. Author interview with "Brian," June 6, 2020, via Webex.

3. Author interview with "Will," April 5, 2021, via Webex.

4. Author interview with "Nicole," April 28, 2021, via Webex.

5. Author interview with "Rebecca," April 9, 2021, via Webex.

6. Author interview with "Duncan," January 2, 2022, via Webex.

7. Author interview with "Angela," March 30, 2021, via Webex.

8. Author interview with "Shelly," May 11, 2021 via Webex.

9. Audrey Clare Farley, "The Eugenics Roots of Evangelical Family Values," *Religion & Politics* (May 12, 2021).

10. George Gilder, *Sexual Suicide* (New York: Bantam Books, 1975).

11. Hilda Løvdahl-Stephens, *Family Matters: James Dobson and Focus on the Family's Crusade for the Christian Home* (Birmingham: University of Alabama Press, 2019).

12. Lynne Gerber, *Seeking the Straight and Narrow: Weight Loss and Sexual Orientation in Evangelical America* (Chicago: University of Chicago Press, 2011).

13. Amy Frykholm, *See Me Naked: Stories of Sexual Exile in American Christianity* (Boston: Beacon Press, 2012), 108.

14. Author interview with "Fay," March 24, 2021, via Webex.

15. Author interview with "Kelli," March 18, 2021, via Webex.

16. Author interview with "Leah," April 15, 2021, via Webex.

17. Author interview with "Lisa," July 14, 2021, via Webex.

18. Author interview with "Jessica," March 14, 2021, via Webex.

19. Author interview with "Angela," March 19, 2021, via Webex.

CHAPTER TWO: POWER AND ABUSE

1. Kelly House, "Sister-in-Law: Ex-MI House Speaker Lee Chatfield Sexually Assaulted Me as a Teen," *Bridge Michigan*, January 7, 2022.

2. Brelyn C. Owens et al., "Purity Culture and Rape Myth Acceptance," *Journal of Psychology and Theology* 49, no. 4 (2021): 405–18; Kathryn Clement et al., "The One Ring Model: Rape Culture Beliefs Are Linked to Purity Culture Beliefs," *Sexuality and Culture* 26 (2022): 2070–2106.

3. Kelly House and Jonathan Ossting, "From the Pulpit, Lee Chatfield's Father Declares 'The Truth Will Come Forward,'" *Bridge Michigan*, January 11, 2022

4. House and Ossting, "From the Pulpit, Lee Chatfield's Father Declares 'The Truth Will Come Forward.'"

5. Sharaya Colter, "True Love Waits Returns to Where It Began," *Baptist Press*, February 7, 2013, https://www.baptistpress.com/resource-library/news/true-love-waits-returns-to-where-it-began-20-years-ago/.

6. Susan Shaw, "A Primer on the SBC's Complicated Relationship with Women," *Sojourners*, June 21, 2013, https://sojo.net/articles/primer-sbcs-complicated-history-women.

7. Christa Brown, *This Little Light: Beyond a Baptist Preacher and His Gang* (Cedarburg, WI: Foremost Press: 2009).

8. Brown published another autobiography, *Baptistland*, which includes a critique of how churches and denominations cover up abuse and target survivors who speak out.

9. Copy of original letter posted on Christa Brown's website Stop-BaptistPredators.org, http://www.stopbaptistpredators.org/documents/Churchresponse.pdf.

10. "Christa Brown: No More Church Secrets About Sex Abuse," *Dallas Morning News*, February 17, 2009, https://stopbaptistpredators.org/documents/Dallas_News_No_more_church_secrets.pdf.

11. *Houston Chronicle*, "Abuse of Faith: The Database," https://www.houstonchronicle.com/news/investigations/abuse-of-faith/database/ accessed March 18, 2025.

12. Kate Shellnut, "Paige Patterson Fired by Southwestern, Stripped of Retirement Benefits," *Christianity Today*, May 30, 2018.

13. Yonat Shrimron, "Paige Patterson's Career Ended After She Came Forward. Her Struggle Continues," Religion News Service, November 21, 2019, https://religionnews.com/2019/11/21/paige-pattersons-career-ended-after-she-came-forward-her-struggle-continues/.

14. Staff, "SWTS: Paige Patterson Terminated 'Effective Immediately,'" *Baptist Press*, May 30, 2018.

15. Julie Myers Wood, Asha Muldro, Bradley L. Dizik, Stephanie Douglas, and Krista Tongring, *Guidepost Solutions' Report of the Independent Investigation of the Southern Baptist Convention*, May 22, 2022, https://guidepostsolutions.com/insights/media-mentions/guidepost-solutions-report-of-the-independent-investigation-of-the-southern-baptist-convention/.

16. Bob Smeitema, "SBC Abuse Reform Task Force Ends Its Work with No Names on Database and No Long-Term Plan," Religion News Service, June 4, 2024.

17. "Abuse Database Is No Long a Priority for Southern Baptist Leaders," Religion News Service, February 18, 2025, https://religionnews.com/2024/06/04/sbc-abuse-reform-task-force-ends-its-work-with-no-names-on-database-and-no-long-term-future-plan/.

18. Emily Joy Allison, *#ChurchToo: How Purity Culture Upholds Abuse and How to Find Healing* (Minneapolis: Broadleaf Books, 2021).

19. Lisa Olsen, Robert Downen, and John Tedesco, "More Than 100 Southern Baptist Youth Pastors Convicted or Charged in Sex Crimes," *Houston Chronicle*, February 13, 2019, https://www.houstonchronicle.com/news/investigations/article/All-too-often-Southern-Baptist-youth-pastors-13588292.php.

20. Richard Ross and Tony Rankin, *When True Love Doesn't Wait* (Nashville: Lifeway Press, 1998).

21. Author interview with "Ann," April 8, 2021, via Webex.

22. Rachel Held Evans, "Do Christian Idolize Virginity?" *Rachel Held Evans* (blog), January 29, 2013, https://rachelheldevans.com/blog/christians-idolize-virginity.

23. Alex Dominguez, "Elizabeth Smart Speaks on Human Trafficking," *Christian Science Monitor*, May 4, 2013, https://www.csmonitor.com/USA/Latest-News-Wires/2013/0504/Elizabeth-Smart-speaks-on-human-trafficking.

CHAPTER THREE: EVANGELICAL EXODUS

1. Blake Chastain, "Exvangelical: A Working Definition," *Post-Evangelical Post*, January 3, 2022, https://www.postevangelicalpost.com/p/exvangelical-a-working-definition.

2. Author interview with "Grace," September 22, 2022, via Webex.

3. Joseph Nathan Cruz, "A Spectacle of Worship: Technology, Modernity and the Rise of the Christian Megachurch," in *Mediating Piety: Technology and Religion in Contemporary Asia*, ed. Francis Khek Gee Lim (Leiden, The Netherlands: Brill, 2010).

4. Chastain, "Exvangelical."

5. Russell Chandler, "'Customer' Poll Shapes a Church: A Minister Discovered Why People Don't Attend. He Founded One of the Nation's Most Successful Congregations," *Los Angeles Times*, December 11, 1989.

6. Author Interview with "Jessica," March 15, 2021, via Webex.

7. Author interview with "Katy," April 28, 2021, via Webex.

8. Author interview with "Roseanne," April 7, 2021, via Webex.

9. Author interview with "Tina," July 11, 2020, via Webex.

10. Author interview with "Keely," June 22, 2020, via Webex.

11. Accounts of the shooting indicate that it was another student, Valeen Schnurr, who was asked by the shooters if she believed in God because she was crying, "Oh my God, my God. Please don't let me die," after being shot. Schnurr survived the attack. Another student in hiding believed this exchange occurred between one of the shooters and Cassie, which led to several months of Cassie being hailed as a Christian

martyr. Dave Cullen, "Why Does the Columbine Myth About 'Martyr' Cassie Bernall Persist?" *New Republic*, September 16, 2015, https://new republic.com/article/122832/why-does-columbine-myth-about-martyr -cassie-bernall-persist.

12. Author interview with "Rose," March 22, 2021, via Webex.

13. Gail Bederman, *Manliness and Civilization: A Cultural History of Gender and Race in the United States* (Chicago: University of Chicago Press, 1995), and Glenna Matthews, *"Just a Housewife": The Rise and Fall of Domesticity in America* (New York: Oxford University Press, 1987.)

14. Author interview with "Joel," June 25, 2021, via Webex.

15. Author interview with "Gabe," June 20, 2021, via Webex.

16. Frank Shyong, "Hate Crime or Not, Atlanta Shooter Motivated by Racism, *Los Angeles Times*," July 30, 2021, https://www.latimes.com /california/story/2021-07-30/shyong-atlanta-shootings.

17. Mark Berman, Brittany Shammas, Teo Armus, and Marc Fisher, "The Atlanta Spa Shooting Suspect's Life Before Attacks," *Washington Post*, March 19, 2021.

18. Rebecca Carroll, "The Charleston Shooter Killed Mostly Black Women. This Wasn't About Rape," *The Guardian*, June 18, 2015.

19. I use the term "color-evasive" rather than the more common "color-blind" due to its ableist implication.

CHAPTER FOUR: CONSTRUCTING THE MYTH
OF WHITE RACIAL IDENTITY

1. Carolyn Fleur-Lobban, *Race and Racism: An Introduction* (New York: AltaMira Press, 2006), 87.

2. For an academic treatment of Blumenbach's work, see Nell Irvin Painter, *A History of White People* (New York: W. W. Norton & Company, 2010). For an undergraduate-friendly explainer, see Franchesca Ramsey, "The Surprisingly Racist History of 'Caucasian,'" *Decoded*, MTV News, April 27, 2016, available on YouTube, https://www.youtube .com/watch?v=GKB8hXYod2w.

3. Quoted in Fleur-Lobban, *Race and Racism*, 87.

4. Takao Ozawa v. U.S., 260 U.S. 178 (1922), available at https:// caselaw.findlaw.com/court/us-supreme-court/260/178.html.

5. United States v. Bhagat Singh Thind, available at https://www .law.cornell.edu/supremecourt/text/261/204.

6. Fay Botham, *"Almighty God Created the Races": Christianity, Interracial Marriage, and American Law* (Chapel Hill: University of North Carolina Press, 2009).

7. Sophie Bjork-James, *The Divine Institution: White Evangelicalism's Politics of the Family* (New Brunswick, NJ: Rutgers University Press, 2021).

8. Public Religion Research Institute, *Support for Christian Nationalism in All 50 States: Findings from PRRI's 2023 American Value's Atlas*, February 2024, https://www.prri.org/wp-content/uploads/2024/02/PRRI -Feb-2024-Christian-Nationalism.pdf.

9. Jesse Curtis, *The Myth of Color-Blind Christians: Evangelicals and White Supremacy in the Civil Rights Era* (New York: New York University Press, 2021).

10. Joe Feagin, *The White Racial Frame: Centuries of Racial Framing and Counter-Framing*, 3rd ed. (New York: Routledge, 2020).

11. Feagin, *The White Racial Frame*.

12. J. C. Mueller, "Racial Ideology or Racial Ignorance? An Alternative Theory of Racial Cognition," *Sociological Theory* 38, no. 2 (2020): 142–69, https://doi.org/10.1177/0735275120926197.

CHAPTER FIVE: SEXUAL PURITY AND RACIAL FORMATIONS

1. Harriet Jacobs, *Incidents in the Life of a Slave Girl, Written by Herself*, ed. L. Maria Child (Boston: Published for the Author, 1861), available at https://www.gutenberg.org/ebooks/11030.

2. Jacobs, *Incidents in the Life of a Slave Girl*.

3. Ida B. Wells, "Southern Horrors: Lynch Laws in All Its Phases," October 5, 1892, at Archives of Women's Political Communication, Carrie Chapman Catt Center for Women and Politics, Iowa State University, https://awpc.cattcenter.iastate.edu/2020/09/21/southern-horrors -lynch-law-in-all-its-phases-oct-5-1892/.

4. Ida B. Wells, "A Red Record," 1895, at Digital History, https://www .digitalhistory.uh.edu/active_learning/explorations/lynching/wells2.cfm.

5. Frances Willard, "A White Life for Two," 1890, available at Archives of Women's Political Communication, Iowa State University, https://awpc.cattcenter.iastate.edu/2020/09/18/a-white-life-for-two -1890/.

6. Frances Willard, "The Race Problem: Miss Willard on the Political Puzzle of the South," interview published in *New York Voice*, 1890, available at "Truth-Telling: Frances Willard and Ida B. Wells," American Association for State and Local History, Truth-Telling: Frances Willard and Ida B. Wells—AASLH, accessed April 8, 2025.

7. Willard, "The Race Problem."

8. Frances Willard, Annual Address to the Woman's Christian Temperance Union (W.C.T.U.) Convention, Cleveland, November 5, 1894, available at https://speakingwhilefemale.co/temperance-willard6/.

9. Wells, "Southern Horrors."

10. Wells, "Southern Horrors."

11. Frances Ellen Watkins Harper, "Social Purity—Its Relation to the Dependent Classes," in *The National Purity Congress: Its Papers, Addresses, Portraits*, ed. Aaron M. Powell (New York: American Purity Alliance, 1896), 328–30.

12. Fanny B. Williams, "Religious Duty to the Negro," in *The World's Congress of Religion; the Addresses and Papers Delivered Before the Parliament and an Abstract of the Congresses Held in the Art Institute Chicago, Illinois, USA, August 25 to October 15, 1893 Under the Auspices of the World's Columbian Exposition*, ed. J. W. Hanson, quoted in Thekla Ellen Joiner, *Sin in the City: Chicago and Revivalism, 1880–1920* (Columbia: University of Missouri Press, 2007), 78.

CHAPTER SIX: SEXUAL PURITY AND RACIAL DISEMBODIMENT

1. Author interview with "Aimee," January 17, 2021, via Webex.

2. In 2004, after significant controversy, the state of Georgia removed all Confederate symbolism from the flag.

3. J. C. Mueller, "Racial Ideology or Racial Ignorance? An Alternative Theory of Racial Cognition," *Sociological Theory* 38, no. 2 (2020): 142–69, https://doi.org/10.1177/0735275120926197.

4. Madison Natarajan et al., "Decolonizing Purity Culture: Gendered Racism and White Idealization in Evangelical Christianity," *Psychology of Women Quarterly* (2022): 1–21.

5. Megan McDonough, "On Love: Brelyn Freeman & Timothy Bowman, Jr.," *Washington Post*, November 20, 2015; Brelyn Bowman, *No Ring No Ting* (Temple Hills, MD: Freeman Publishing, 2016).

6. Author interview with Kaisha Esty, September 8, 2023, via Webex.

7. Michelle Mitchell, *Righteous Propagation: African Americans and the Politics of Racial Destiny after Reconstruction* (Chapel Hill: University of North Carolina Press, 2004).

8. Crunk Feminist Collective, "Single, Saved, and Sexin': The Gospel of Getting Your Freak On," February 3, 2011, https://www.crunkfeminist collective.com/2011/02/03/single-saved-and-sexin-the-gospel-of-gettin -your-freak-on/.

9. Crunk Feminists, "Single, Saved, and Sexin'," March 15, 2013, at YouTube, https://www.youtube.com/watch?v=ejKj9Ii6q9E.

10. Brittney Cooper, *Eloquent Rage: How a Black Feminist Found Her Superpower* (New York: St. Martin's Press, 2018).

11. Brittney Cooper, "Grown-Woman Theology: Lessons of Race, Blackness, and Power from a Self-Described Nerdy Black Girl,"

Longreads, March 2, 2018, https://longreads.com/2018/03/02/grown
-woman-theology/.

12. Crunk Feminists, "Single, Saved, and Sexin'."

13. Crunk Feminists, "Single, Saved, and Sexin'."

14. Evelyn Brooks Higginbotham, *Righteous Discontent: The Women's Movement in the Black Baptist Church, 1880–1920* (Cambridge, MA: Harvard University Press, 1993).

15. Author interview with Monique Moultrie, May 4, 2023, via Webex.

16. Jasmine Holmes, "Growing Up Black in the Purity Movement," author website, January 10, 2018, https://jasminelholmes.com/purity
-culture-black-women/.

17. Lyz Lenz, "Recovering from I Kissed Dating Goodbye: A Roundtable," *The Toast*, June 8, 2016, the-toast.net/2016/06/08/recovering
-from-i-kissed-dating-goodbye-aroundtable/.

18. All essays in this forum curated and published by Lomax can be found here: https://thefeministwire.com/?s=%23Blackskinwhitesin.

19. Tamura Lomax, "#BlackSkinWhiteSin: The Black Church, Black Women, and Sexual Discourses of Resistance," TheFeministWire.com, February 13, 2017, https://thefeministwire.com/2017/02/blackskinwhitesin
-black-church-black-women-sexual-discourses-resistance-revised/.

20. Monique Moultrie, *Pious and Passionate: Religious Media and Black Women's Sexuality* (Durham, NC: Duke University Press, 2017).

21. Monique Moultrie, "From Free to Freaks: Analyzing Juanita Bynum's Dilemma of Holy and Ho, The Feminist Wire," TheFeminist Wire.com, February 14, 2017, https://thefeministwire.com/2017/02/black
skinwhitesin-free-freaks-analyzing-juanita-bynums-dilemma-holy-ho/.

22. MiHee Kim-Cort, "I Am a Scholar of Religion. Here's What I See in the Atlanta Shootings," *New York Times*, March 24, 2021.

23. Angie Hong, "The Flaw at the Center of Purity Culture," *The Atlantic*, March 26, 2021.

24. Anna Beahm, "The Racist Links Between Purity Culture and Christian Nationalism," *Reckon News*, November 8, 2022.

25. Mark Berman, Brittany Shammas, Teo Armus, and Marc Fisher, "The Atlanta Spa Shooting Suspect's Life Before Attacks," *Washington Post*, March 19, 2021.

26. Samuel L. Perry, *Addicted to Lust: Pornography in the Lives of Conservative Protestants* (New York: Oxford University Press, 2019).

27. MiHee Kim-Cort, "Asian Women, Christianity, and American Purity Culture," teaching module, Center for Religion & the Human, Indiana University, https://crh.indiana.edu/engaging-religion/teaching
-modules/kim-kort-module.html, accessed January 21, 2025.

28. Hong, "The Flaw at the Center of Purity Culture."

29. Amir Vera, "Church Removes Atlanta Shooting Suspect from Its Membership," March 21, 2021, https://www.cnn.com/2021/03/21/us/crabapple-first-baptist-church-atlanta-spa- shootings/index.html.

30. Comedian Sabrina Wu addresses the problematic nature of the book *Tikki Tikki Tembo* regarding the Chinese language in her stand-up routine, available at https://www.youtube.com/watch?v=GJlNK 7x5iWs.

CHAPTER SEVEN: MYTHS AND MARTYRS OF WHITE CHRISTIAN NATIONALISM

1. J. C. Mueller, "Racial Ideology or Racial Ignorance? An Alternative Theory of Racial Cognition," *Sociological Theory* 38, no. 2 (2020): 142–69, https://doi.org/10.1177/0735275120926197.

2. Robin Bernstein, *Racial Innocence: Performing American Childhood from Slavery to Civil Rights* (New York: New York University Press, 2011), 6.

3. James Baldwin, *The Fire Next Time* (New York: Vintage Book, 1963), 101.

4. Instagram, Brenz Marie, https://www.instagram.com/brenzmarie.

5. Brenda Davies, *On Her Knees: Memoir of a Prayerful Jezebel* (Grand Rapids, MI: Eerdmans, 2021), 99.

6. Alice Greczyn, *Wayward: A Memoir of Spiritual Warfare and Sexual Purity* (Austin, TX: Greenleaf Book Group, 2021), 331.

7. Martin Luther King Jr., *Strength to Love*, 1963 (Boston: Beacon Press, 2019).

8. Ruby Hamad, *White Tears/Brown Scars: How White Feminism Betrays Women of Color* (New York: Catapult, 2020).

9. Ruby Hamad, "How White Women Use Strategic Tears to Avoid Accountability," *The Guardian*, May 8, 2018, https://www.theguardian.com/commentisfree/2018/may/08/how-white-women-use-strategic-tears-to-avoid-accountability.

10. Alice Greczyn, "The Photo: How a Girls' Getaway in Joshua Tree Became a Symbol of White Supremacy and Why I'm Not Here to Do Better," author website, November 15, 2021, https://www.alicegreczyn.com/blog/the-photo-how-a-girls-getaway-in-joshua-tree-became-a-symbol-of-white-supremacy.

11. Devorah Margolin and Hilary Matfess, *The Women of January 6th: A Gendered Analysis of the 21st Century American Far Right*, Program on Extremism, George Washington University, 2020, https://extremism.gwu.edu/women-january-6th.

12. Samuel Braslow, "The 'Beverly Hills Insurrectionist' and the Big Myth About Jan. 6," *Rolling Stone*, May 21, 2023, https://www.rolling stone.com/politics/politics-features/gina-bisisnano-jan6-beverly-hills -insurrectionist-1234739137/; Samuel Braslow, "Beverly Hills Salon Owner Recounts Her Action in D.C. Riot," *Beverly Hills Courier*, January 14, 2021.

13. Braslow, "Beverly Hills Salon Owner Recounts Her Action in D.C. Riot."

14. Tucker Carlson, "A Death in the Capitol, and What We Must Do Now," Fox News.com, January 6, 2021, https://www.foxnews.com /opinion/tucker-carlson-capitol-hill-riots-reaction.

15. Vera Burgengruen, "'Our First Martyr.' How Ashli Babbitt Is Being Turned into a Far-Right Recruiting Tool," *Time*, January 10, 2021, https://time.com/5928249/ashli-babbitt-capitol-extremism/.

16. Jenna Ryan, @realennaryan, Twitter, March 26, 2021, https:// twitter.com/dotjenna/status/1375443216720400387?lang=en; Rachel Weiner, "She Said She Wasn't Going to Jail for Jan. 6, Citing 'Blonde Hair White Skin.' A Judge Sentenced Her to 60 Days Behind Bars," *Washington Post*, November 4, 2021, https://www.washingtonpost.com /local/legal-issues/jenna-ryan-jail-capitol-jan-6/2021/11/04/c94cd8c2 -3d82-11ec-8ee9-4f14a26749d1_story.html.

CONCLUSION

1. Linda Greenhouse and Reva B. Siegel, "Before (and After) *Roe v. Wade*: New Questions About Backlash," *Yale Law Journal* 120, no. 8 (2011): 2031, http://www.jstor.org/stable/41149586.

2. To get started with this growing body of literature, see Rebecca Wolfe, "How Purity Culture Impacted My Eating Disorder: In My Religious Community My Body Was Labeled a Risk," *Medium*, July 8, 2019, https://medium.com/the-salve/how-purity-culture-impacted-my -eating-disorder-1edac61fa4ce; Sandra Nobel and Hilary McBride, "Appetites and Arousal: Disruptions of Embodiment in Purity Culture," presentation at the International Association of Eating Disorders, 2023, https://iaedp.confex.com/iaedp/2023/meetingapp.cgi/Session/5655; and Rebecca Wolfe and Rebekah Vickery, "Graham Crackers and Good Girls: A Historical and Theoretical Case for Expanding the Conceptual Reach of Purity Culture's Control of Bodies Assigned Female at Birth," *Theology & Sexuality* 29, nos. 2–3 (2024): 92–108, https://doi.org/10.1080 /13558358.2024.2332984.

3. Gene Gemby, "The Truth Behind the Lies of the Original 'Welfare Queen,'" *Code Switch*, NPR, December 20, 2013, https://www.npr

.org/sections/codeswitch/2013/12/20/255819681/the-truth-behind-the
-lies-of-the-original-welfare-queen.

4. Edward McClelland, "The True Story of Chicago's Welfare
Queen," *Chicago*, May 16, 2019, https://www.chicagomag.com/city-life
/may-2019/the-true-story-of-chicagos-welfare-queen/.

INDEX

abortion, 144

abstinence. *See* sexual abstinence

acquaintance rape, 38

Affiliated Christians, 65, 72–74

After Purity Project, 4–5, 8–9, 10

Against Purity (Shotwell), 5

AIDS Memorial Quilt, 2–3

Allison, Emily Joy, 46–47

American Broadcasting Corporation (ABC), 3

American Civil Liberties Union (ACLU), 91–92

American Progress (Gast), 7, 102

Amish, 29

Anderson, Laura, 52–53, 54

anti-Asian violence, 77–78, 123–26

anti-miscegenation laws, 11, 91–92

anti-racism, 93–94

Arterburn, Stephen, 26

Aryans, 87, 89–90

Asian women and womanhood, 77–78, 123–25

authoritarianism, 32–33

autonomy, 99, 101, 102, 116

Babbitt, Ashli, 13, 140

Baldwin, James, 130

beauty, 136

Beef (TV series), 61–62

Bernall, Cassie, 73

Bernstein, Robin, 130

Bessey, Sarah, 54

Bisignano, Gina, 139–40

Bjork-James, Sophie, 92–93

Black Lives Matter movement, 9, 10, 68, 81, 94–95

Black men: anti-Black violence against, 79–81; anti-miscegenation laws and, 11, 91–92; fears of sexuality of, 79; lynchings, 11, 24, 91, 103–4, 107; as threats to White women's purity, 102–5

Black Panthers, 95

Black purity culture, 115–23

#BlackSkinWhiteSin, 121–22

Black women and womanhood: bodies of, 120; evangelical purity culture and, 117–23; exploitation of by White men, 11, 98–101; protection of purity by, 102, 116; slavery and enslavement, 98–101

"Blue Lives Matter", 80–81

173